CHRISTMAS For Quilters

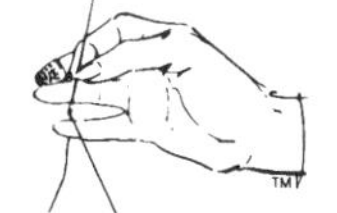

BETTY BOYINK PUBLISHING • 818 Sheldon Road • Grand Haven, Michigan 49417

Printed in U.S.A.

Introduction . . .

There's just something about Christmas! Whether quilts or patchwork or other hand-made delights, holiday projects bring joy to the maker/giver and appreciation to the recipient.

Christmas red can be poppy, scarlet, crimson, cranberry, strawberry, cherry, tomato, garnet, ruby, or claret. Christmas green can be hunter, kelly, grass, lime, or teal. And isn't it interesting that most people can pick out that special hue either in red or green that speaks of Christmas to them. It can change over the years as the manufacturers of Christmas goods and fabrics emphasize various hues.

The true brighter red and green will always be Christmas, or the more recently popular deep burgundy red and the dark hunter green. Often, just using red and green colors will cause a quilt to be called a Christmas quilt. But do Christmas quilts have to be red and green? We think not! Some quilts in this book are not the usual colors of Christmas, but still denote Christmas by their design. Just check out the color photographs.

Christmas designs are included on these pages: the Nativity scene complete with wisemen and shepherds, a Church, angels, dove, cardinal, Santa Claus, Twelve Days of Christmas, tree, poinsettia, and the list goes on. Quilters have added their array of designs and ideas to the listing, such as the pine tree, holly, poinsettia, bow ribbons, specially designed stars, etc.

Bed quilts to wall quilts, holiday decorating accents for the table, under the tree, and those ever popular stockings that need decorating are featured on the following pages.

There are two sets of quilts that should be checked out. One is the set of three very different holiday quilts from guest quilters where we explore the creative process on pages 40-41. The second set of quilts is the story of the six quilters who shared in a round robbin type of project. They used some of the special holiday fabrics from Hoffman California Fabrics, Fasco Fabric Sales Co, and RJR Fashion Fabrics. We were pleasantly surprised with the way the plaid fabrics blended and complemented the metallic prints or holiday prints in the pieces that developed as they were exchanged from one quilter to another. These quilts are on pages 31-33. Experience the result of a creative challenge!

Each quilter selected a 12 inch block design from twelve offered ... some pieced, some appliqued. Using a pre-chosen package of fabric, the first quilter made the block and then sent it on to a second quilter for her to add to the block. A third quilter added additional touches, and a fourth quilter made sure that piece was a finished quilt top complete with borders. Fifth and sixth quilters did the quilting. In this way, we did not end up with another project to quilt!

Try doing a special project like this with your friends using the holiday designs offered. It is a giving way to enjoy the sharing of quiltmaking and the Holiday Season.

****

About The Author

When Betty started quilting in the early 1970's, she began experimenting with as many of the traditional blocks as possible. Each new quilt grew into an adventure with what happened when design, color and fabric all came together. Over the last few years, the designs of the holiday season have occupied much of her time as the samples were made for illustrating ideas, patterns and results of the folk lore research.

Betty Boyink Publishing was formed as a means of sharing the knowledge and designs of quiltmaking. A whole series of theme pattern books have been published to accomplish this goal. A 12 and 18-inch size tablet of graph paper were added to the product line because of the lack of suitable products for quilters to draft patterns. Later, a line of plastic templates was added as quilters wanted to speed up the process of quiltmaking.

She is honored to have a bicentennial skirt at the Smithsonian Institute, Washington, DC. After designing a special Bicentennial Star quilt pattern, she was invited to the White House to present President Gerald Ford a quilt in the oval office.

Betty is a National Quilting Association Certified Teacher, having served several years on the Certification Committee. She lectures, teaches and shares her quilting enthusiasm throughout the U.S., Canada and Europe. Beginning in 1981, she organized the North Woods Retreat and continues to develop and teach new themes for participants each year. As one of the original challenged in 1987, she annually coordinates the Hoffman Challenge with Holice Turnbow. Appointed to organize a national quilt contest/show to help celebrate the U.S.Coast Guard 200th Anniversary, the show took place July 1990. She had over 100 of her quilts featured in a one woman show at the Holland, Michigan Tulip Festival exhibit in 1992.

Living in Michigan, the snow covered wonderland provided a wealth of design inspirations, photograph opportunities and time to stitch. ENJOY!

List of Previous Publications

Baskets for Quilters - 52 pages with 39 patterns 4,8 & 12"
Child's Play for Quilters - 60 pages, includes pieced ABC's
Creating Memory Quilts - 80 pages, 50 color photo/ideas
authored by Madonna Ferguson
Double Wedding Ring Design - 68 pages, 5 sizes, strip pieced
Fans Galore for Modern Quilters - 68 pages, 32 projects
Flower Gardens & Hexagons - 60 pages, 54 blocks
Michigan Quilters - 52 pages, 21 heritage blocks, 17 new
co-authored with Milly Splitstone
Nine Patch Design Adventures - 72 pages, 44 projects
Nautical Voyages for Quilters - 72 pages, 7 size Compass etc.
Quilt Challenges - 72 pages, Explore phenomenon!
Quilters Hearts w/ Ribbons - 58 pages, Mostly "heart" designs
Star Quest for Quilters - 80 pages, 98 stars in 4, 8, 12"
Trees & Leaves for Quilters - 60 pages, 40 tree/10 leaf blocks

A Special Thank You ...

to three very special daughters!

and for all of the quilters who share a love of making the holidays special with those quilted pieces. Thanks to the five other Holiday Quilters: Linda Gabrielse, Sue Nicholson, Pat Nordmark, Jaynet Peters,and Milly Splitstone. Creativity was shared by Guest Artist Marge Etter, Gail Hunt and Judy Pierce. A special thanks to Debbie Cadwallender, Janice Godlov, Jackie Huizen.

In Memory

Christmas at the Boyink home has many cherished memories Holiday time 1993 will be a very different time as we adjust to the loss of one very special Son, Husband, Dad, Grandpa, Good Friend, Confident, and Partner . . . Brent A. Boyink.

Table of Contents

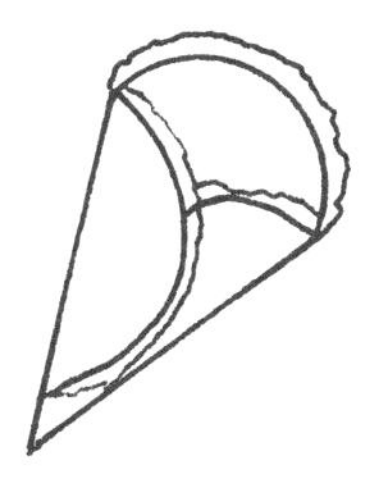

Cone Ornament:

One of the simple early ornaments that is quite easy to make today and just as elegant on the tree is a cone shape. It was often of lace or fabric with lace edging added, therefore often called a Victorian era tree ornament. Let's make this project the way it might have been made in the early days of ornament making. Draw around the edge of a saucer (gives that perfect 6" diameter shape without even thinking whether diameter is across center of circle or around outer edge or circumference). Cut out circle shape. Add a lining if very delicate fabric used. Stitch lace on outer edge using a zig-zag catching lining and outer fabric. Edge is finished as you stitch on lace. Fold in cone shape. Allow top to open up which closes bottom of shape.

Now comes the fun! Decorating the cone shape further (possibly with a ribbon at the overlap), beads, sequins, buttons, etc. Then fill with baby's breath and dried flowers per Victorian era or use your imagination with all that is available today.

Country Church

12 inch Block

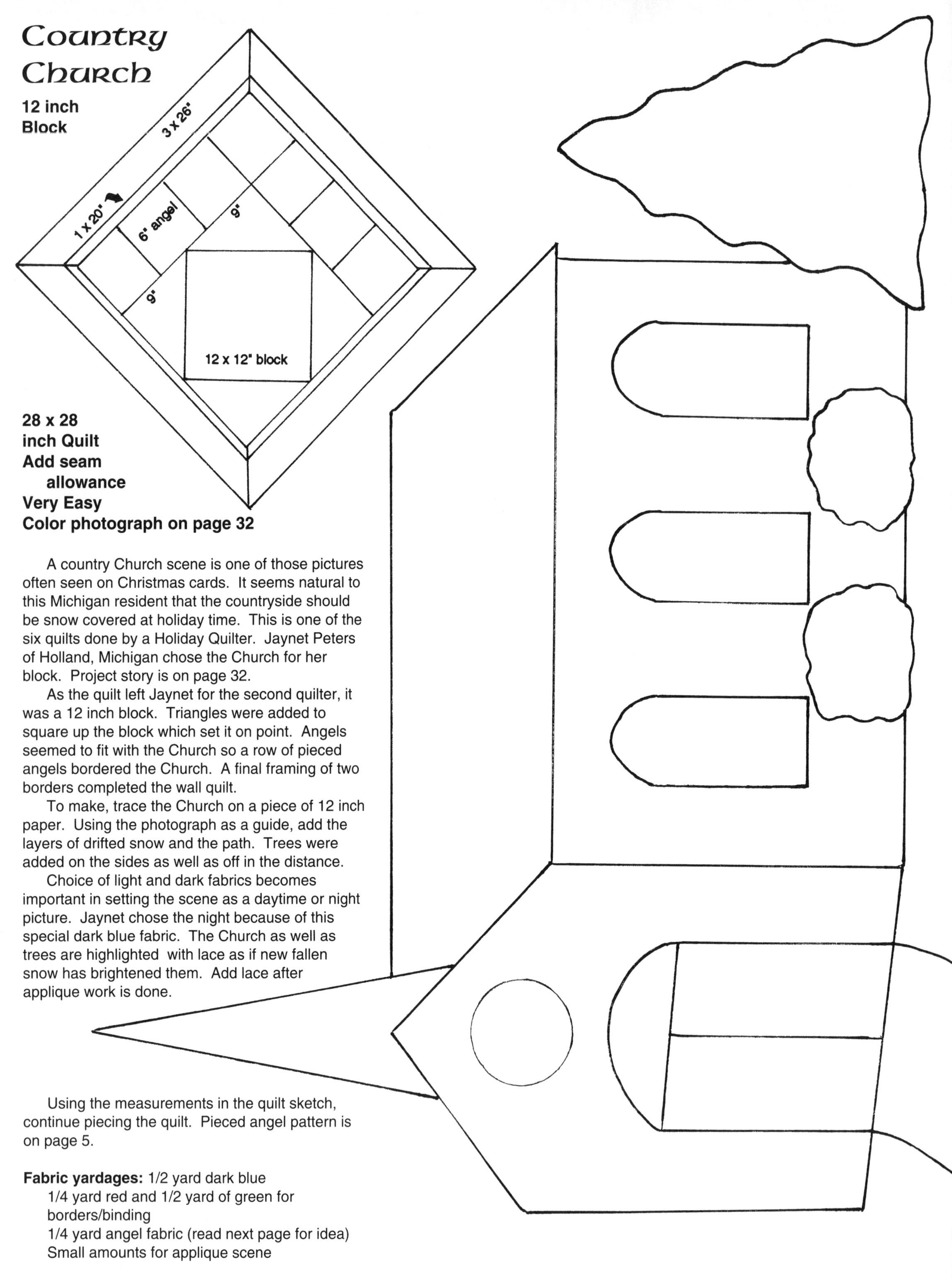

28 x 28 inch Quilt
Add seam allowance
Very Easy
Color photograph on page 32

A country Church scene is one of those pictures often seen on Christmas cards. It seems natural to this Michigan resident that the countryside should be snow covered at holiday time. This is one of the six quilts done by a Holiday Quilter. Jaynet Peters of Holland, Michigan chose the Church for her block. Project story is on page 32.

As the quilt left Jaynet for the second quilter, it was a 12 inch block. Triangles were added to square up the block which set it on point. Angels seemed to fit with the Church so a row of pieced angels bordered the Church. A final framing of two borders completed the wall quilt.

To make, trace the Church on a piece of 12 inch paper. Using the photograph as a guide, add the layers of drifted snow and the path. Trees were added on the sides as well as off in the distance.

Choice of light and dark fabrics becomes important in setting the scene as a daytime or night picture. Jaynet chose the night because of this special dark blue fabric. The Church as well as trees are highlighted with lace as if new fallen snow has brightened them. Add lace after applique work is done.

Using the measurements in the quilt sketch, continue piecing the quilt. Pieced angel pattern is on page 5.

Fabric yardages: 1/2 yard dark blue
1/4 yard red and 1/2 yard of green for borders/binding
1/4 yard angel fabric (read next page for idea)
Small amounts for applique scene

Angels

6 inch Pieced / actual size applique
Add seam allowance, Medium

As the celestial messengers between God and man, Angels foretold the story of the birth of Christ. They alerted the shepherds to the miraculous birth and how to find the Christ child by following the star. There is a song in their honor . . . *Hark! the Herald Angels Sing . . .* with words written in 1730 by Charles Wesley. Pealing of the Church bells on Christmas morning was his inspiration. It was not set to music until 1810 when Dr. Cummings of Walthan Abbey fitted it to the familiar tune by Mendelssohn. The final combination was published in 1856.

We have both a pieced and an appliqued angel for your holiday projects. The smaller 6-inch size block seemed fitting for many holiday projects. The circle head is appliqued on with the halo embroidered on a 2 x 2 inch square (cut 2-1/2 x 2-1/2 inches to include seam allowance). The pieced angel was used as a bordering effect for the Church on page 4. To give the ever lightening effect upward, the row of angels was made from a dark, medium and light fabric in same shade. For that lacy effect, a see through lace was used over the solid cotton color underneath.

Hark! The Herald Angels Sing
Hark the herald angels sing - Glory to the new-born King!
Peace on earth and mercy mild, Gold and sinners reconciled!
Joyful all ye nations rise Join the triumph of the skies;
With the angelic host proclaim Christ is born in Bethlehem!
Hark! the herald angels sing Glory to the new born King.

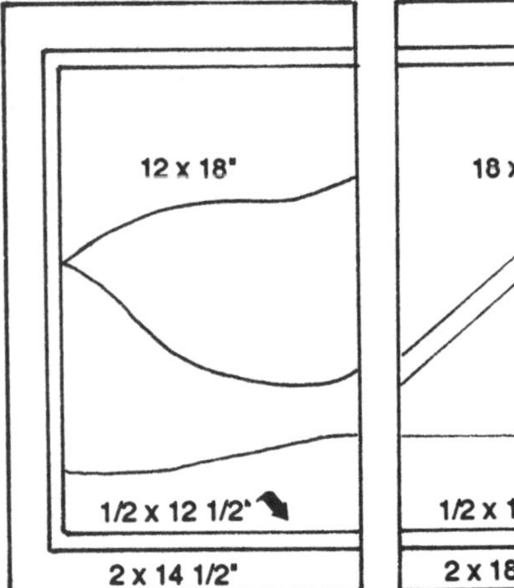

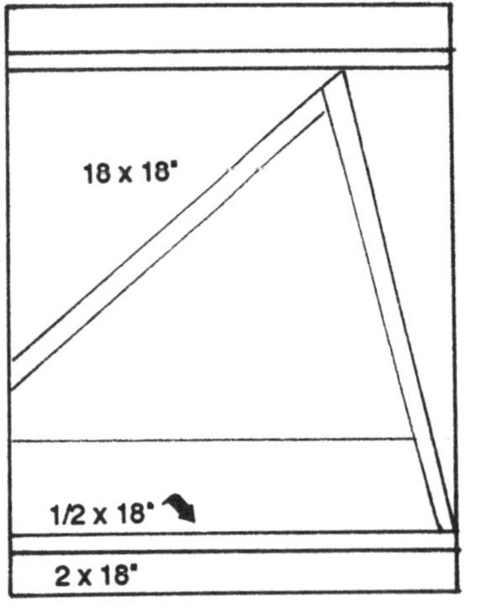

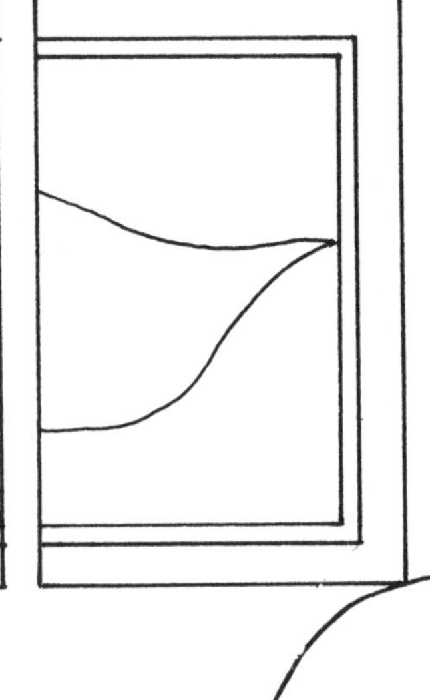

The Nativity

3 panels, 18 x 18 inches, 12 x 18 inches
Add seam allowance, Medium
Shown in color on inside front cover

A three panel design will help quilters achieve their goal of producing Christmas pieces. Set a goal of achieving one panel each month. Start with the larger one in October, smaller two panels in November and December when busier days are upon us.

Note that the border flows around the outer edge of the three combined pieces. The center edge of the wall quilt grouping is finished into itself so that there is no interruption of design even with a binding.

To make, take a piece of 18 x 18 inch paper to set the scene for center panel, 12 by 18 inch for outer two panels. Using the measurements in the sketch of the quilt, draw in the lines for the stable effect. Note that the outer edge of each stable line flows to the outer two pieces as the line continues in that piece. The lines create a flow back and forth between the three separate panels to make them one visual image. Use sketch above as a guide, or you may decide to make each panel a solid piece of fabric.

Dark fabric creates the night time star field with the lighter fabric illumination from within the stable. A floor line was created by using many fabrics of similar depth of color in 1 inch and 3/4 inch widths ... angled off from the shape given on page 7.

Let us pass along an applique tip that was used in several of the designs in this piece as well as others throughout this book. If the piece being appliqued in place has several parts, it is faster and easier to piece as much as possible, then applique the whole shape in position. For example, machine stitch the longer lines to the parts for the garments of Joseph, Mary and the Wisemen. By using several shades of the same color family, the illusion of folds and depth is achieved in these garments. Take a look at the color photograph to see this technique in more detail. Areas of light to dark shading help to achieve greater depth for that more realistic look to the figures.

Faces! Choose a way to give definition to the lines in the faces. Fine embroidery of the facial features works, or you may elect to use the permanent pins for drawing the human lines giving a pen and ink look. These can be crucial in bringing the figure to lifelike images. Human warmth, personality and characteristics are difficult to achieve in the fabric medium. Hands are a single piece of skin tone fabric with the fingers divided by embroidery lines or markers.

The star pattern is given on page 7. Here is another example of where parts are pieced together and then appliqued in position. If appliquing points are a problem for you, you may choose to piece the points into position. After drawing the star shape in position on the paper, take a ruler, marking straight from star point out to outer edge of block. This means the background area is pieced rather than a single layer of fabric with the star appliqued in place. It gives the same finished look without the frustrations of appliquing those fine points.

Continued on Page 7

Continued from Page 6

The three individual panels could be included in one piece by sewing a 1 inch sashing between the three. Continue to assemble, quilt and bind off.

Should you want to add an Angel to the three piece nativity scene, check page 5 for a pattern.

Fabric requirements:
1-1/4 yards backing,
1 yard of outer border,
1/2 yard inner border
At least three shades of the color chosen for each garment
Small amounts for applique, floor boards,
3 golds for star
Background fabric or prepare to piece

Three Wisemen

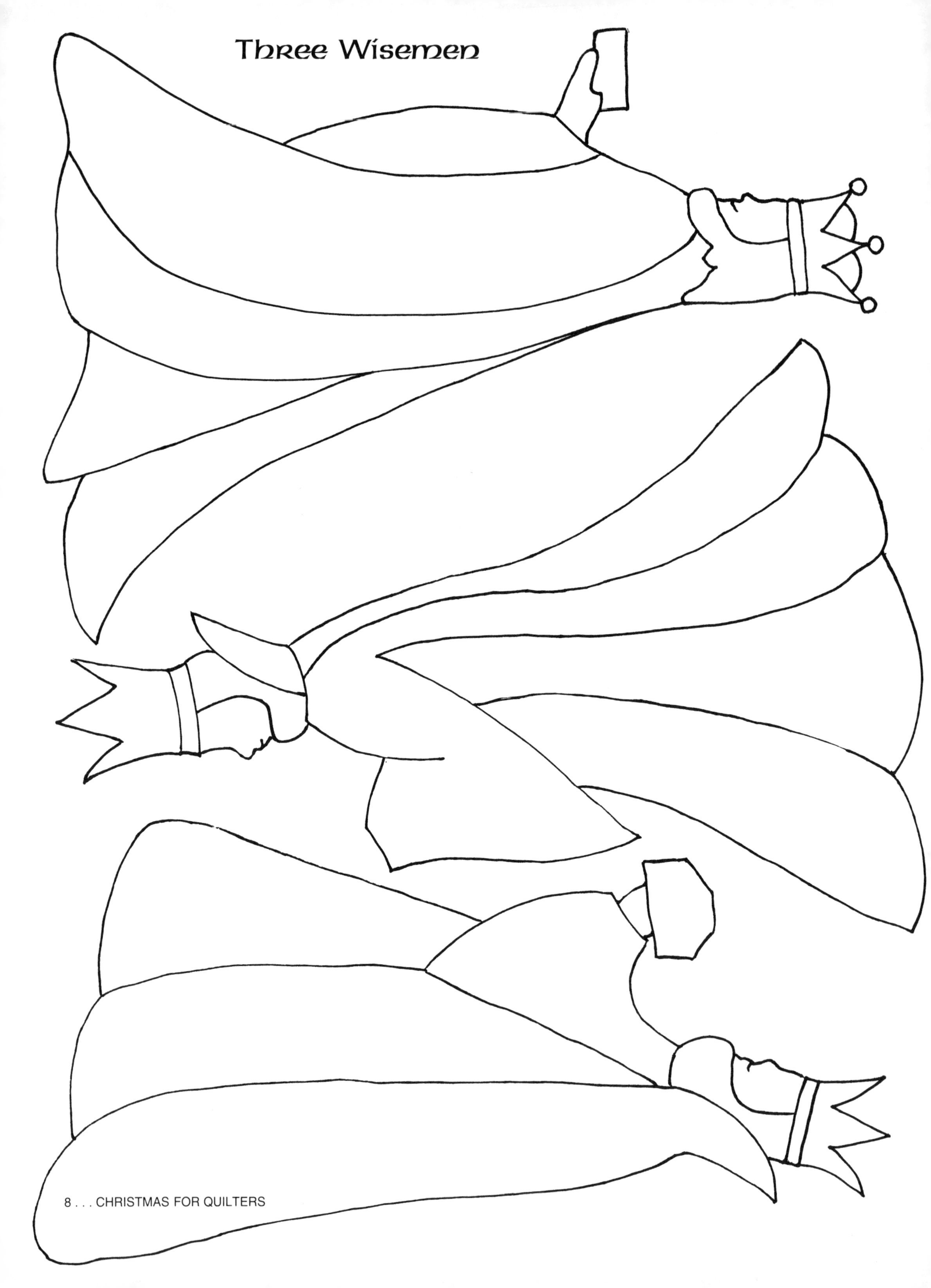

Santa Through The Windows Of Time

Quilt sketch on page 10.

There is probably no more universally accepted gift giver than the one that has become known as Santa Claus to Americans. He did not appear overnight, but through many centuries of faces and changes in appearance. The folk lore continues to evolve as each new generation adds their artistic interpretations.

Let's take a look back in time at some of the customs, traditions, costumes and writings that caused the changes that have brought us to the present. After careful study of the available material of an elusive part of our folk history, a quilt was designed that helps make the "Santas through time" come to life. The quilt as pictured on the back cover focuses in on four old world Santas, the American idea of Santa on the rooftop, the "pencil" Santa of the 1990's as well as that helpful little elf.

Let's look at Nicholas from the time of Saint through evolution to Santa Claus. Only a little over 200 years after Christ's birth, in the village of Patara in Turkey, an early Christian couple ... Epiphanes and Johane were married for many years without children. Their prayers were answered with a son, whom they named Nicholas. While a young man, his parents died from a plague, leaving Nicholas a small inheritance. The young man shared love and his inheritance with the village people giving gifts of food, clothing or money anonymously.

He became the Bishop of Myra because of his faith and good deeds. One story tells of Nicholas helping feed his people during a famine with the help of ship captains who donated portions of their cargo. Yet at unloading time, the full measure of grain was aboard. Another story tells of his tossing a bag of gold coins through a poverty stricken friend's window for a dowry for one of three daughters. A second bag was tossed. When the third bag was tossed the noise awakened the father enabling him to catch the elusive benefactor. It is this story that makes some artists portray Nicholas with three bags of gold.

Nicholas died around A.D. 343 December 6. The day was set aside in honor of the man whose good works and deeds lived on in the hearts of the people he had served. He became a patron saint not only in his area, but throughout the Netherlands. The image of this saint changed as the stories spread.

Holland customs kept St. Nicholas, but added a white horse and helper in the form of Black Peter. He was a devilish character with horns who slid down chimneys delivering presents to good children and birch rods to the naughty ones. Children set out wooden shoes on December 5 for collecting goodies. Shoes were also set out on Church alters to collect for distributing to the poor in St. Nicholas' name.

In northern Germany, Nicholas became known as Pelze Nichol or fur-clad Nicholas, losing his bishop's robes. The German children also set out shoes for filling. German children placed notes in shoes to be delivered to Christkindl, the Christ Child.

By the mid 1500's, Protestant churches under the leadership of Martin Luther denounced the worship of saints, especially St. Nicholas. During the 1600s, the day of gift ving had been changed in many countries to December 25 denoted as Christmas Day.

In England, after St. Nicholas Day was no longer recognized, Father Christmas took over the role of gift giver.

The Dutch, German, and other cultures that migrated to the new world brought their customs of honoring St. Nicholas on December 6, Father Christmas on Christmas Eve, as well as the image of the gift givers. In the first Dutch settlement in New Amsterdam, the robes of St. Nicholas were shed in lieu of the clothing of the men of 1600s. The Dutch name was Sinter Claes, with a change in appearance to a short and chubby figure over the tall, thin Saint Nicholas figure. He wore a flat, board-brimmed hat and smoked a long Dutch pipe. As the nationalities intermarried, Father Christmas and Sinter Claes blended into Santa Claus.

Continued on Page 15

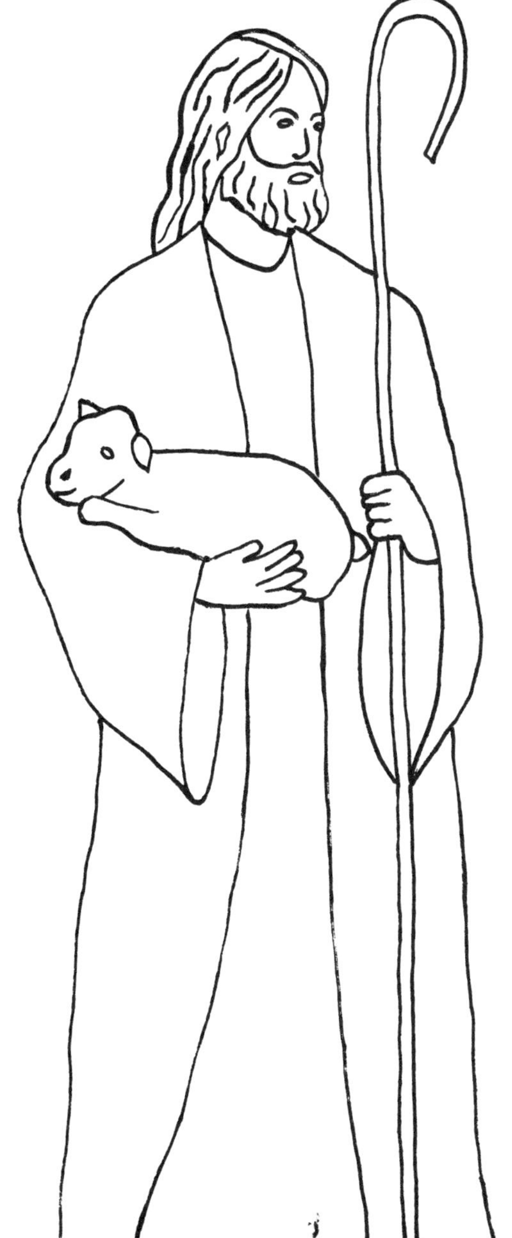

Shepherds from Nativity Scene on page 6. Santa designs begin on page 10.

3 1/2 x 42"
12" 9" 12" 12"
12" 19 3/4" 3/4 x 17" 3/4 x 15"
9" 1/2 x 21
3 1/2 x 42" 10 x 11"
25"
1 x 25" 1 x 25"
1 x 12" 1 x 12"

Santa Through The Windows of Time

42 by 44 inches, 12 inch blocks
Add seam allowance, Difficult
Shown in color on back cover

Seven Santa figures are illustrated. Four historical Santas were positioned through windows as if back in time, an elf collects gifts in the attic, the American Santa image of today waits to take off from the rooftop, and the newer image of a pencil Santa hovers by the chimney.

The Santa drawings follow on pages 10 through 15. Remember to add seam allowance. Position Santas on background blocks using measurements in sketch of quilt, again adding seam allowance. Added dimension of color was achieved by the use of some non-traditional quilt fabrics... such as ultra suede for shoes/gloves for those small angles with difficult to turn under edges. No turn under is required on ultra suede. Fur-like fabric was used where fur is called for; also to make beards. The use of velvets/corduroy or other nap type fabrics can give more dimension by using the nap of the fabric for darker/lighter areas. Faces are embroidered. Gold braid and other trims add that regal touch of elegance required.

The clothing was machine pieced together, then appliqued by hand as if one piece. This proved to save time.

Continued on Page 11

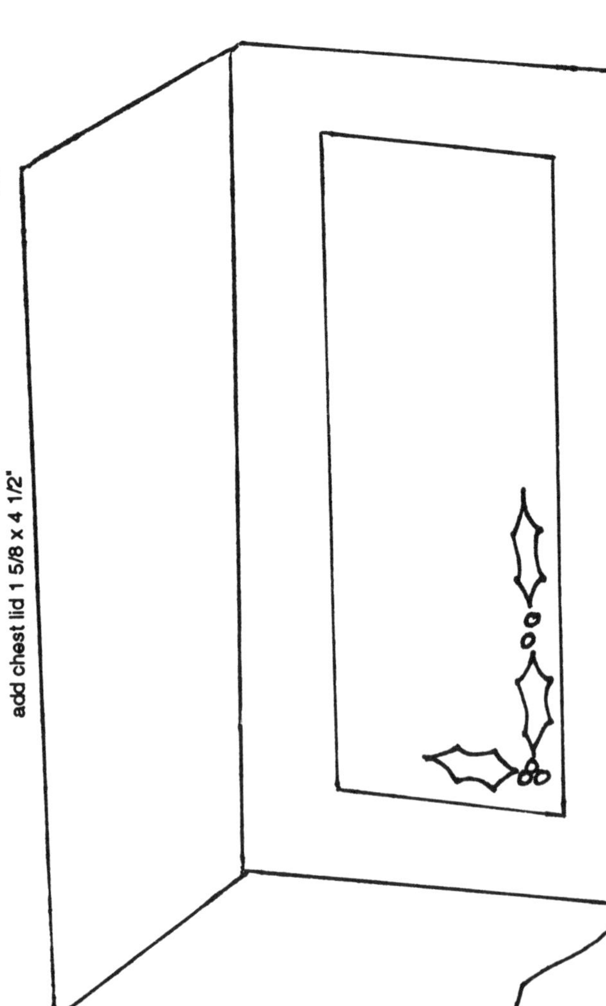

Continued from Page 10

Add normal applique seam allowance, taking same seam allowance as you sew pieces together. Press in direction that gives the look of over/under depth the design requires. Start with pieces toward back building upwards to front for depth emphasis. If trims are needed in seams, attach trim before sewing seams. Piece blocks and add frames. Attic area was pieced totally before adding Santa, Elf and chimney. Use measurements to piece chimney end of house. Draw out on paper, cut apart, and add seam allowance as you cut fabric.

Fabric requirements:
1/2 yard background
1/2 yard house print
1/4 yard light/dark window divider strips
1/4 yard chimney
1-1/4 yards borderprint
small amounts for applique

Kris Kringle... a German toy maker who carries a Christmas tree with his bag of toys for good little children. The idea of the Christmas tree originated in Germany more than five hundred years ago.

Father Christmas...English Father Christmas was an early Christian monk who was especially kind to people. He is known to have travelled on foot putting treats in good children's stockings hung by their fireplaces at Christmas time.

Pencil Santa... a more recent addition to the Santa story; the tall, slim Santa carries a wreath. Many of the typical characteristics of the red outfit, white fur, long beard and mustache have the same look as our more traditional Santa Claus.

Saint Nicholas... The Dutch St. Nicholas takes its origin from the Bishop of Myra. The Saintly image includes a crown and cephre. He is often illustrated in red robes. More detailed information is in narrative story of Santa on page 9.

Papa Frost . . . was modeled after the Czars of history and fairy tales. He pulled a sleigh full of toys, sugarplums and fruited cakes. Traveling during the Northern Lights, Papa Frost would hide the treats all over the house for the little ones to find. His fur lined coat is made from shades of blue to give that frosty look to this gift-giver.

Continued from page 9

The German immigrants brought to the United States their gift giver, the Christkindl or Christ child. As the customs intermixed, Kriss Kringle emerged resembling fur clad Nicholas.

The Swedish gift giver, Jultomte, was more of an elf image. Jultomte wore a red hat and had a long white beard.

The first person to write for posterity about St. Nicholas in the newly formed United States was Washington Irving of New York City. In his novel, *A History of New York from the Beginning of the New World to the End of the Dutch Dynasty*, Irving under the pseudonym of Diedrich Knickerbocker, describes St. Nicholas dressed in traditional Dutch attire. Irving suggested St. Nicholas flew over rooftops dropping presents down chimneys.

American Santa Claus... descriptions from Clement Moore's *'Twas the Night Before Christmas* give Americans their image of Santa Claus. Red suit trimmed in white fur with a black belt and black boots made a colorful image for early prints when color was added to the printing process. A bag of toys is a big part of the image. See addition of reindeer on title page.

Professor Clement Moore, also of New York City, gave the more modern look to Santa Claus with the poem written for his children in 1822, as he described St. Nicholas:

"He had a broad face and a round little belly
That shook, when he laughed, like a bowl full of jelly.
He was chubby and plump --a right jolly old elf,
and I laughed, when I saw him, in spite of myself."

Thomas Nast, cartoonist for Harper's Weekly Magazine, aided the transformation of the Bishop of Myra, St. Nicholas to the jolly old elf, Santa Claus with his pen and ink drawings. For 23 years beginning in 1863, Nast drew a new Santa for each holiday season. It was his drawings that gave Santa the home workshop at the North Pole.

St. Nicholas/Santa drawings had always been in black and white until color printing in the late 1800s when Nast chose seven drawings to put in color. A vibrant red was chosen for Santa's suit since it would look bright in print.

The next artist to make a change was Haddon Sundblom who in 1931 when illustrated the Coca Cola advertisement Santa. Santa was shown as a full grown man, no longer an elf!

Through the years the Santa figure we recognize today evolved. Is the "pencil" Santa a figment of the imagination of an artist of the 1990's, adding yet a new dimension to an ageless story? Going back about 1700 years to Saint Nicholas, Bishop of Myra, devotion to God continues to inspire the spirit of giving ... emerging as a folk hero.

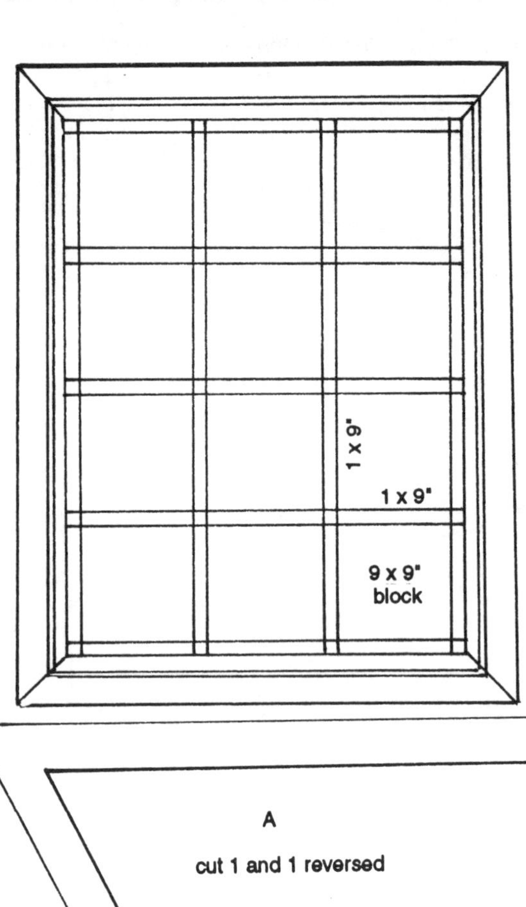

Pieced Santa

38 by 48 inches quilt, 9 inch block
Add seam allowance, Easy
Shown in color on inside back cover

A pieced Santa Claus? Yes, and it's quick and easy to assemble so you have time for more projects. This design was drawn with the idea of strip piecing some details rather than working with such small pieces. The basic Santa is there ... ready to have those special touches that give a personality to the character. A beard is made of wool, eyes/nose/mouth details are embroidered, ball fringe is used for pompoms, and little black buttons are placed down the front.

The six-piece Christmas tree block is about the simplest stylized tree shape possible. The tree is decorated with 1/8 inch red ribbon garland attached periodically with a pearl bead over a sequin. A soft, toned-down light green print background is used in both blocks.

Make templates of each shape required. The leg is one template cut over three strip pieced colors (cut 3-1/4 inch red, 3/4 inch white, and 1-1/4 inch black strips). Strip measurements include seam allowance. The arm can also be one template (cut 3-3/8 inch red and 1-3/8 inch white strips).

Continued on Page 17

Fabric requirements:
- 1 yard light green background/border
- 1-1/2 yards tree/border/binding
- 1/3 yard red Santa/corners/border
- 1/4 yard sashing print
- 1/4 yard white
- 1-1/2 yards backing

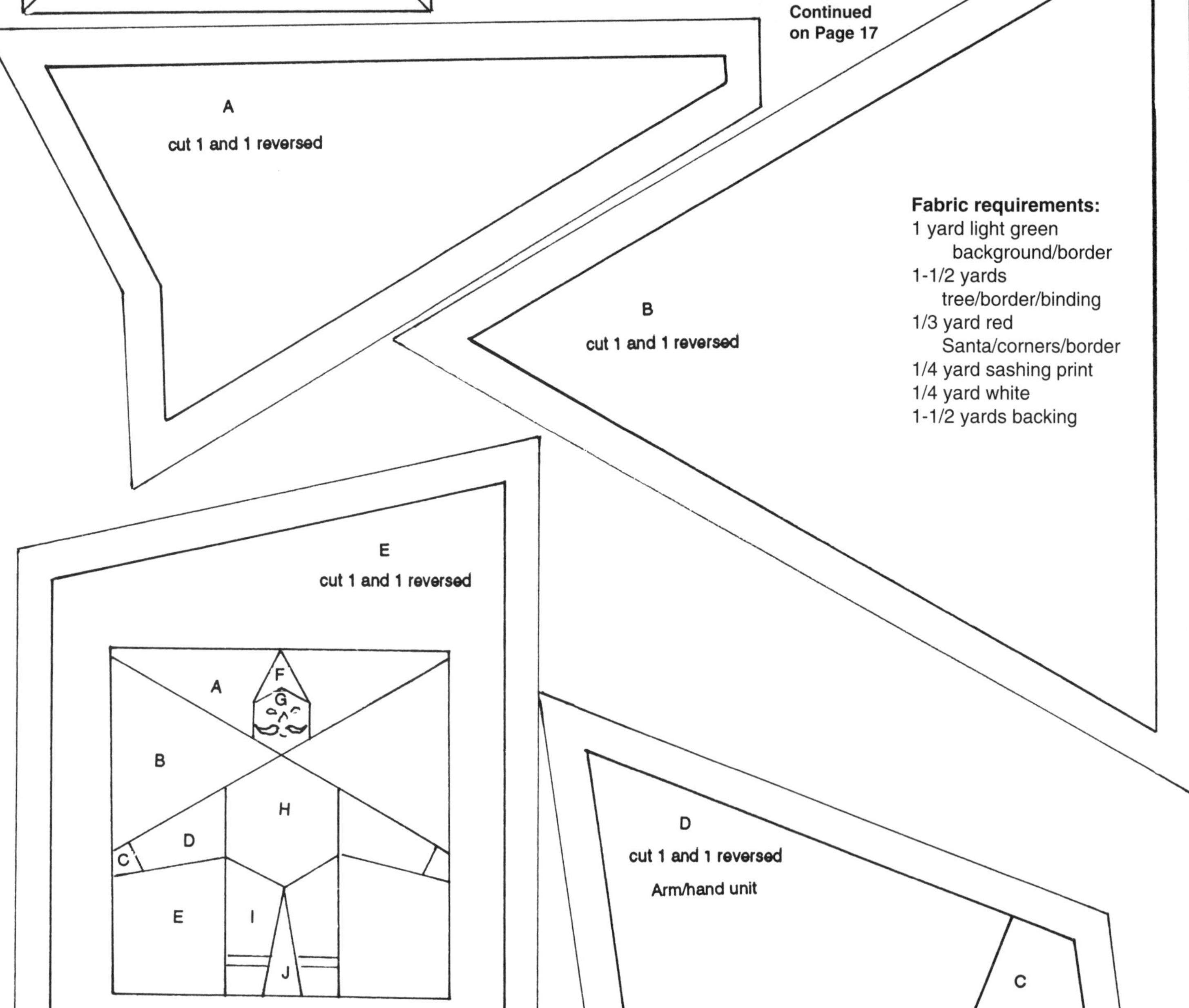

Contined from Page 16

The white down center front and across bottom of jacket hexagon is made of 1 inch white bias. When using bias down front, press under 1/3 of each side and applique in position. Add buttons. For across bottom, fold in half and press. Sew in position as you sew hexagon to legs.

Once six Santa blocks are all stitched and personalized, six tree blocks are stitched and decorated, assemble in rows. Note 1 inch sashing divides the blocks. The red intersection squares help tie the color together and promote eye movement back and forth across piece. Using sketch on page 16, add three borders.

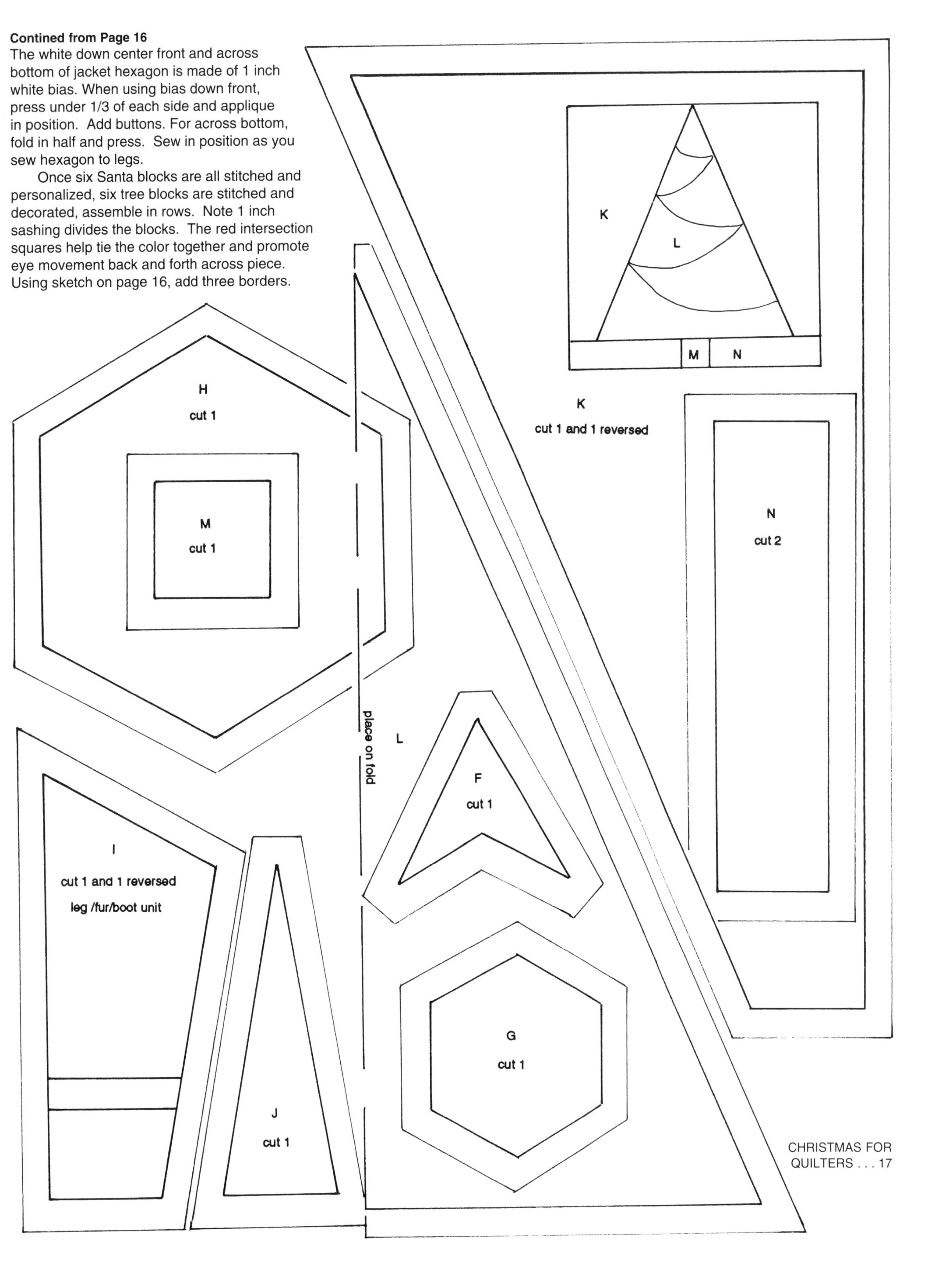

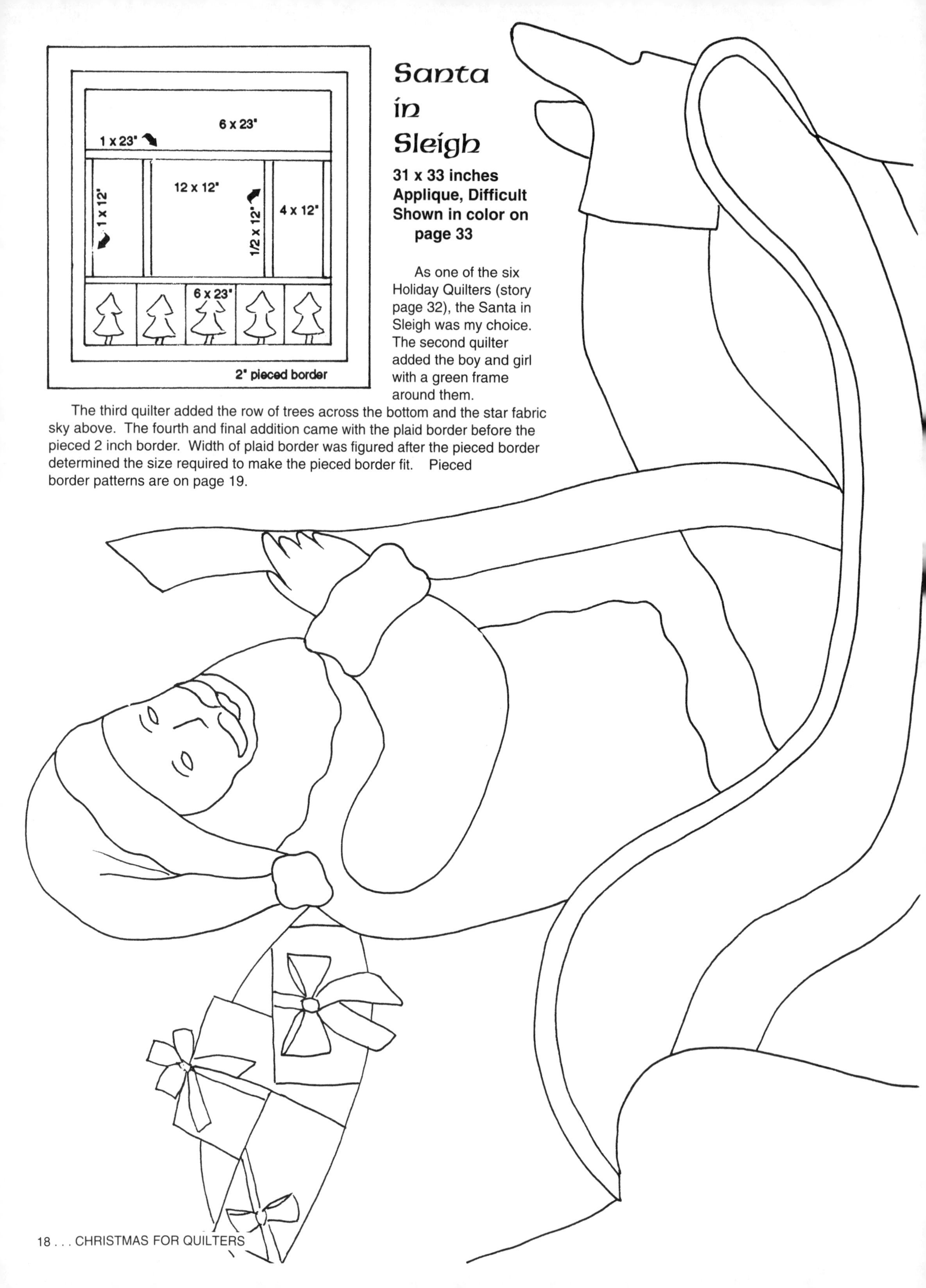

Santa in Sleigh

31 x 33 inches
Applique, Difficult
Shown in color on page 33

As one of the six Holiday Quilters (story page 32), the Santa in Sleigh was my choice. The second quilter added the boy and girl with a green frame around them.

The third quilter added the row of trees across the bottom and the star fabric sky above. The fourth and final addition came with the plaid border before the pieced 2 inch border. Width of plaid border was figured after the pieced border determined the size required to make the pieced border fit. Pieced border patterns are on page 19.

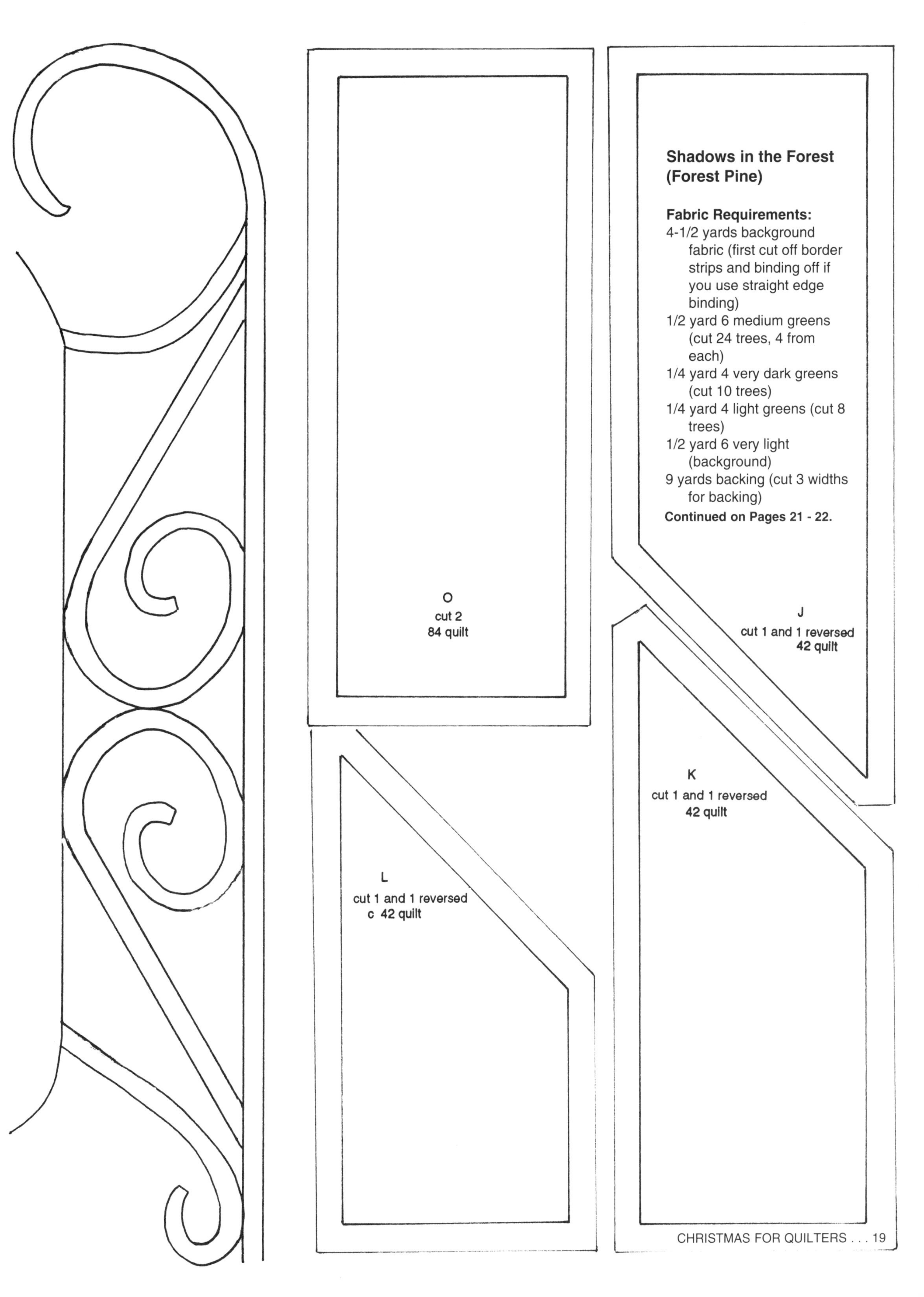

Shadows in the Forest (Forest Pine)

Fabric Requirements:

4-1/2 yards background fabric (first cut off border strips and binding off if you use straight edge binding)

1/2 yard 6 medium greens (cut 24 trees, 4 from each)

1/4 yard 4 very dark greens (cut 10 trees)

1/4 yard 4 light greens (cut 8 trees)

1/2 yard 6 very light (background)

9 yards backing (cut 3 widths for backing)

Continued on Pages 21 - 22.

Shadows in the Forest

89 x 101 inches, 12 inch block
Add seam allowance, medium
Shown in color on page 35

Fabric requirements on page 19. Patterns on pages 19 - 21. Block on page 22.

It is often difficult to catch scenes from nature in fabric, but the specially designed tree pattern here seems to portray the layered boughs of the pine tree to perfection. It is achieved using the ever decreasing shape upwards, dividing each section at an angle as it moves through the layers of the tree. A single block is sketched on page 22.

One of the delightful visions of the quilt is that the darker trees show forth. Looking closely we see that the quilt could be reversed because the lighter opposite shape also forms a tree block. Another fun part of this design is the ability to assemble it in rows across the quilt. It does require laying out the entire quilt, especially if you plan to do some shading with a light source. Imagine a bright light shining down through the quilt...now make this area with lighter colored fabrics. You also need to use lighter shades in light color range as well.

A busy green/brown print was selected for the border and the main tree pieces (patterns 1, 3, 5, 7, and 9). Many other greens with similar depth of color were used for pattern pieces 2, 4, 6, and 8. This gives a good strong tree image yet aids in the layering look of the boughs. Make 42 blocks (24 medium, 10 very dark and 8 light). These light blocks need to be darker than the lighter background fabrics so that trees are pronounced..

Consider eliminating seams between blocks by cutting pattern pieces 10, 11, 12, 13, 14 and 15 as one. To make template for the new shape, simply lay these pattern pieces on the fold. It is much more accurate to make a template rather than using fold for each shape. You still need to make 10-15 templates because they are used on outer edges.

A caution here reminds us that the pattern shapes are one way shapes, and cannot be multiple cut with right sides together. If you are going to multiple cut, be sure you cut all the shapes with right sides of fabric facing up. Also indicate "up" on template so that it doesn't get turned over as you are cutting.

Continued on Page 21

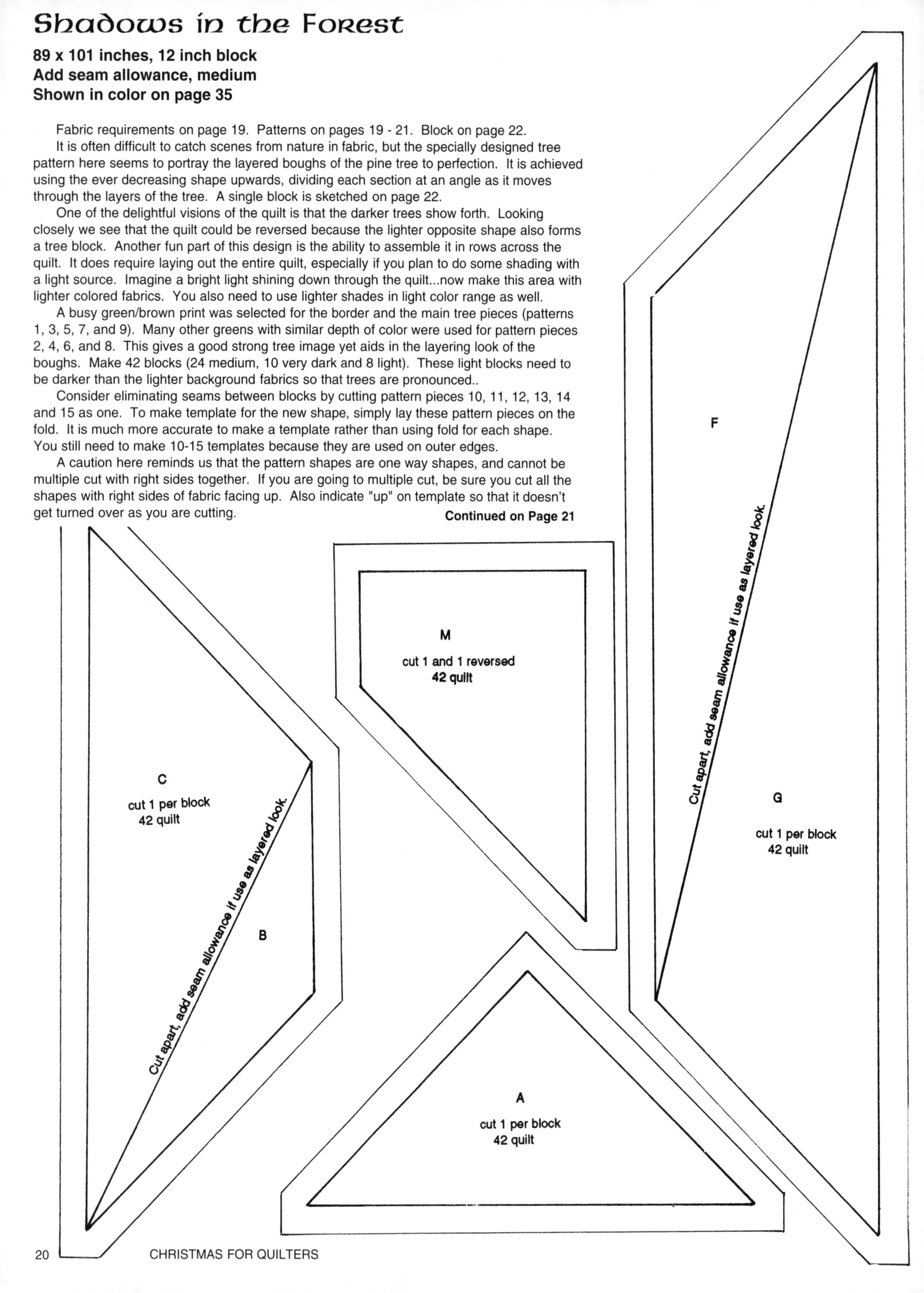

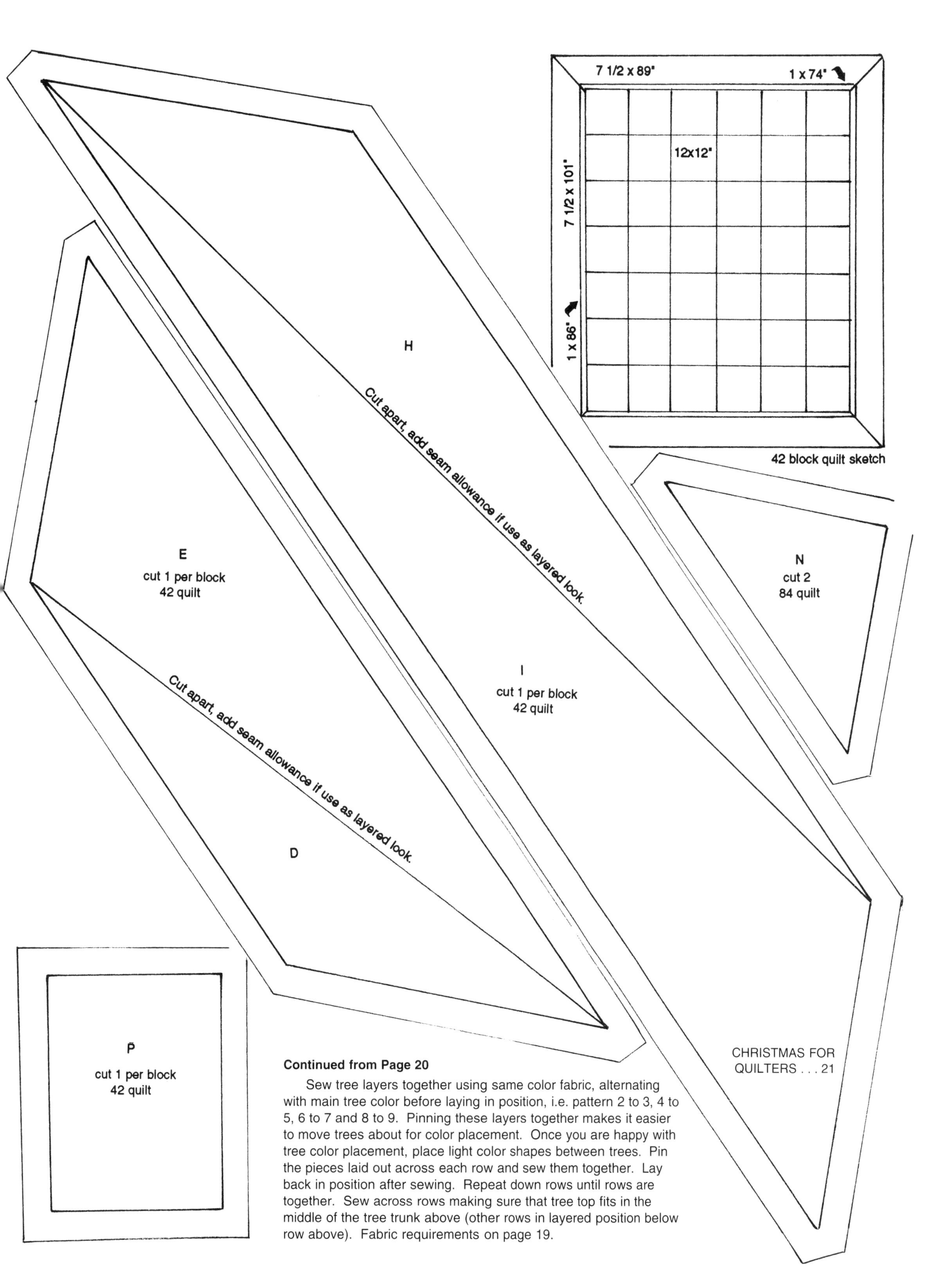

Continued from Page 20

Sew tree layers together using same color fabric, alternating with main tree color before laying in position, i.e. pattern 2 to 3, 4 to 5, 6 to 7 and 8 to 9. Pinning these layers together makes it easier to move trees about for color placement. Once you are happy with tree color placement, place light color shapes between trees. Pin the pieces laid out across each row and sew them together. Lay back in position after sewing. Repeat down rows until rows are together. Sew across rows making sure that tree top fits in the middle of the tree trunk above (other rows in layered position below row above). Fabric requirements on page 19.

Forest Pine

12 inch block
Add seam allowance, Medium
Shown in color on page 35

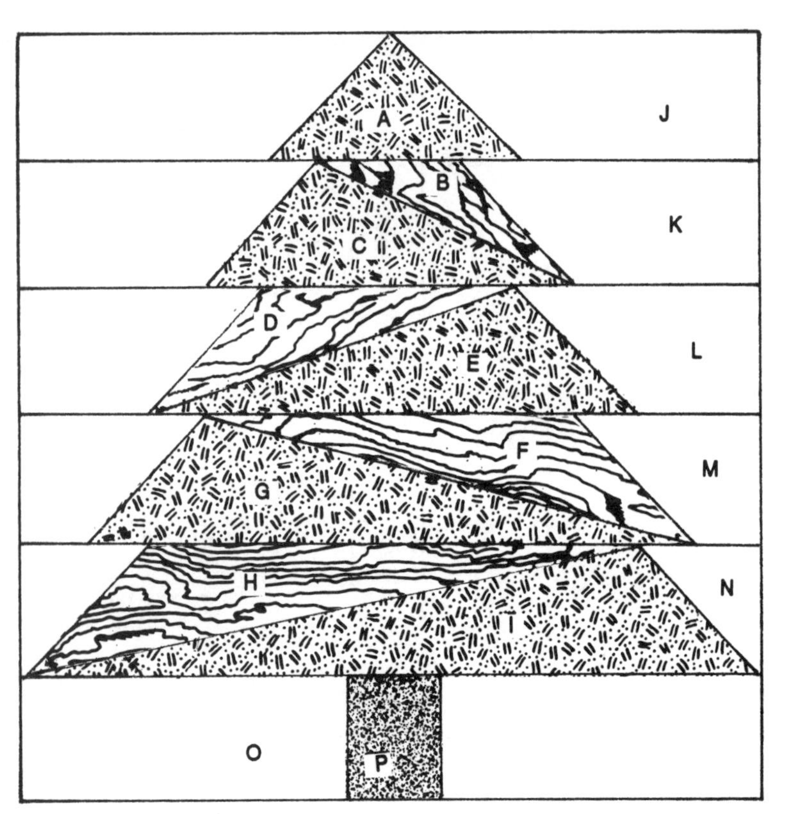

Memories of visual scenes help to determine a name for a newly designed quilt block. Having grown up in the Shenandoah Valley at the foothills of the Blue Ridge Mountains in Virginia, the view of trees abound. The move to the sandy shores along Lake Michigan brought out the lack of trees and forest. Of course I had seen pine trees over the years and even studied all types of trees when working on the book TREES & LEAVES FOR QUILTERS (Betty Boyink) published 1982. But a recent trip to the northwest part of the country brought quite a different visual perspective on "the pine tree". Awesome, grandeur, magestic, the adjectives continue so easily! There were forests of tree after tree, tall and layered like the shape this tree represents.

I've labeled the block "medium" difficulty because of the tapered lines that go to a sharp point. Just sew the two parts of the lines together, i.e. B to C, D to E, and so on before sewing rows of trees together. You may choose to make just 5 pieces for each tree.

Two Forest Pine blocks combined with two triangles are all it takes to make a holiday table runner. Any of the other 12 inch tree blocks may be substituted for the block design. Use the measurements in the sketch to make the triangles, remembering to add seam allowance. The triangles made a good spot to add ruche' pine cones and pine needles. Pine needles help fill in around the pine cones. These may be embroidered for that fine line look required. Pattern pieces are on pages 19-21

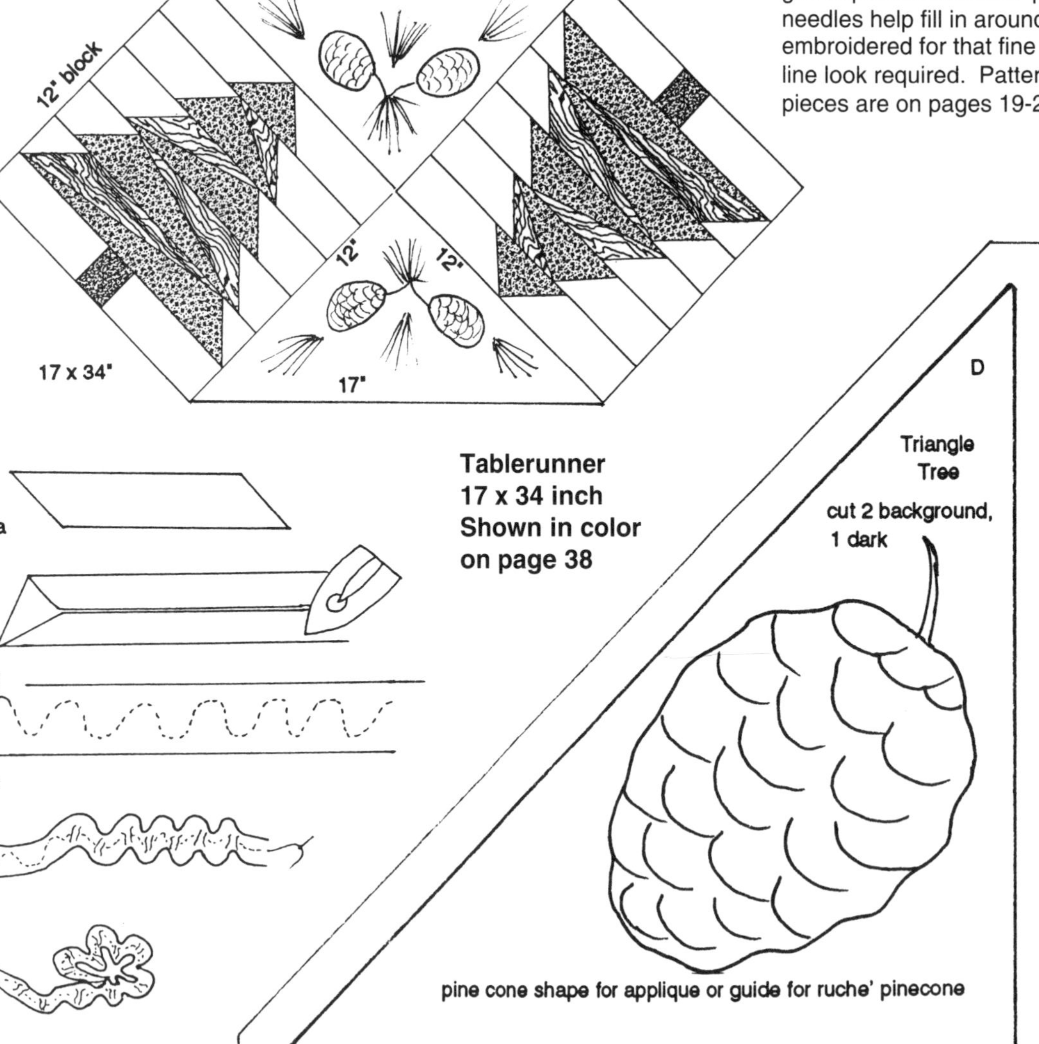

Tablerunner
17 x 34 inch
Shown in color on page 38

To make the pine cone using the ruche' technique, follow the steps below:

a. Cut a piece of bias fabric 24 inches long by 2 inches wide.
b. Fold under 1/2 inch on each side and press.
c. Run a curved gathering thread either by hand or by machine. This thread will stay in the work so you should match the color of the fabric exactly.
d. Pull gathering thread so that strip evenly gathers.
e. Begin at the center of the pine cone and applique the edges down ... circling the center in ever widening shapes until the oval pine cone is complete. Tuck in the raw edges of the last row as you stitch in position the outer edge. A visual example of the technique is shown.

Triange Tree - cut 1 C

Triangle Tree

12 inch block
Add seam allowance, Medium
Shown in color on page 34

A beautiful, delicate tree is made up of many, many triangles. There are two variations given for the base of the tree. A 12 inch tree block was used in the Gift Wrap wall quilt sketched on page 27. You can make this block by piecing together two triangles to form a square, and squares together to form rows. Using the illustration of the block, piece top four rows of triangles together. Piece remaining triangle rows and add to trunk section before combining the two sections. Pattern pieces C and D are on page 22.

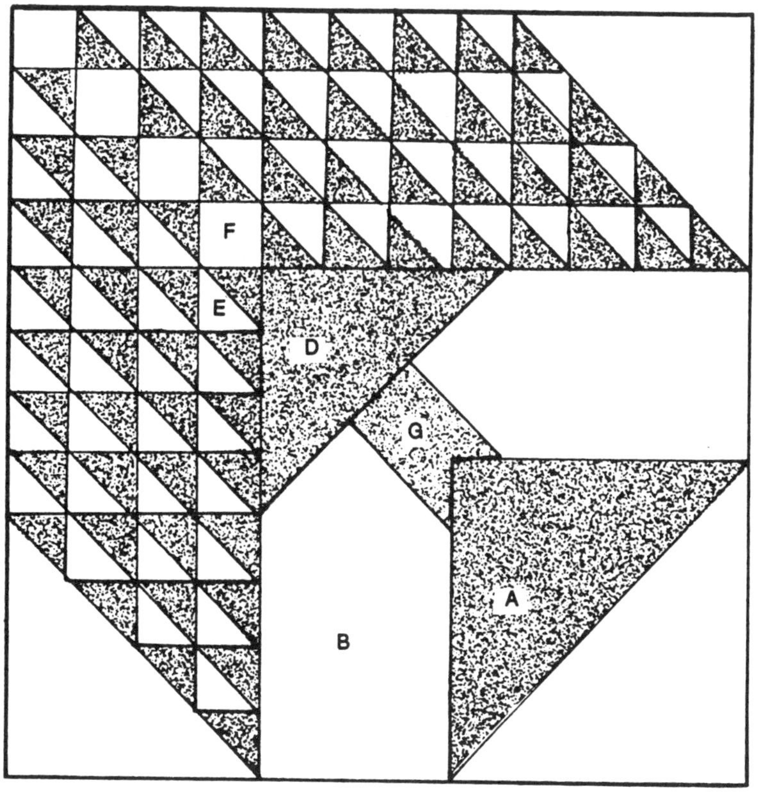

F
E
D
G
A
B

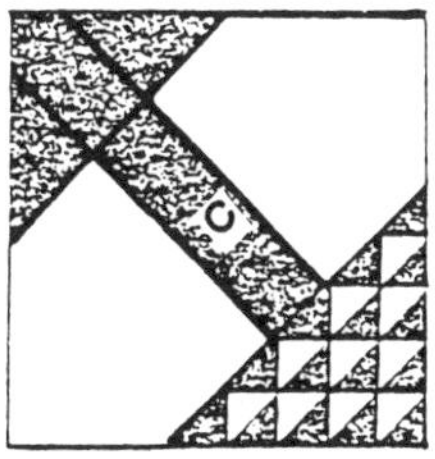

C

tree trunk variation

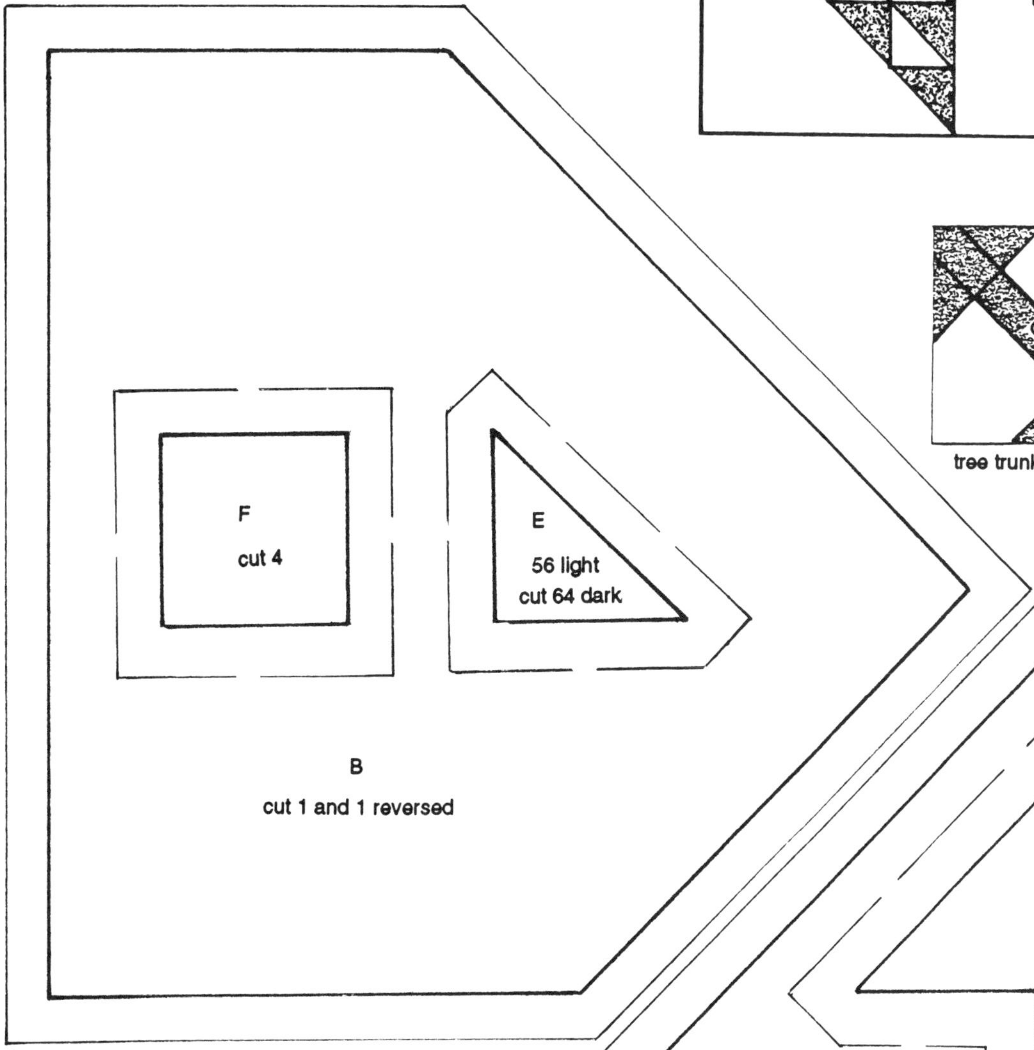

F
cut 4

E
56 light
cut 64 dark

B
cut 1 and 1 reversed

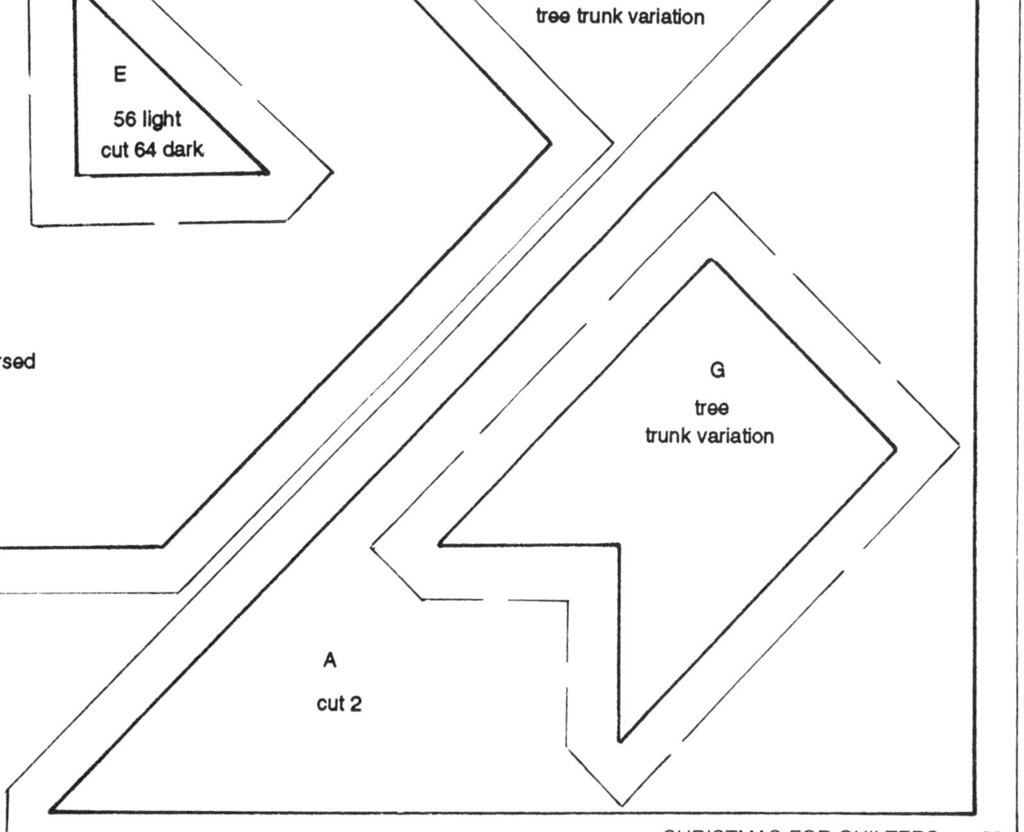

G
tree
trunk variation

A
cut 2

Pine Tree Quilt

93 x 110 inches, 12 inch block
Add seam allowance, Easy
Shown in color on page 35

Thirty of the most popular tree blocks made with triangles will make a quilt. Set on point, which sets the trees upright on the bed. Note diagonal direction of individual block illustrated on the opposite page. The tree blocks are often set with alternating solid blocks for an area of quilting. A touch of color may be added by using this very simple alternating block. The openness allows individual tree block to be prominent. Note the block has a perfect area for a flowing leaf quilting motif illustrated on the pattern piece.

My preference of many fabrics within the similar color range resulted in yet another quilt. Pulling out the greens in my collection easily gave me many different shades for the trees and that touch of color in alternating blocks.

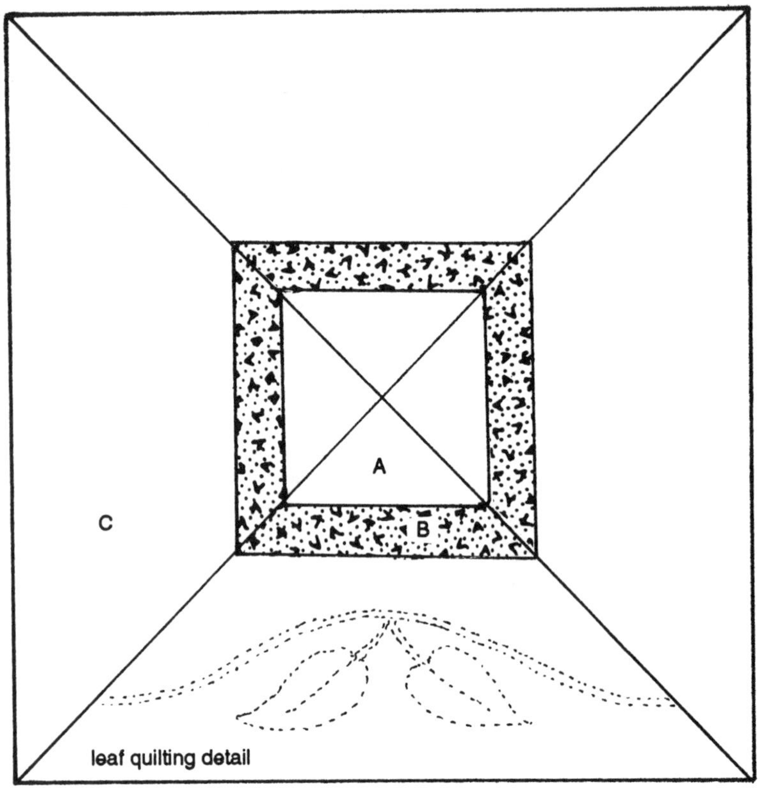

Pattern pieces for the tree block on page 25 include the two sizes used in projects in the book ... 8 and 12 inch. The 8 inch block was used in wall quilt seen in color top of page 38, while the 12 inch block was required for the full quilt. Please take note that the alternating block on page 24 has seam allowance included, but the pattern pieces on page 25 of the pine tree do not. It was necessary to not include seam allowances to have all pattern pieces included. Add the 1/4 inch seam allowance as you make your template.

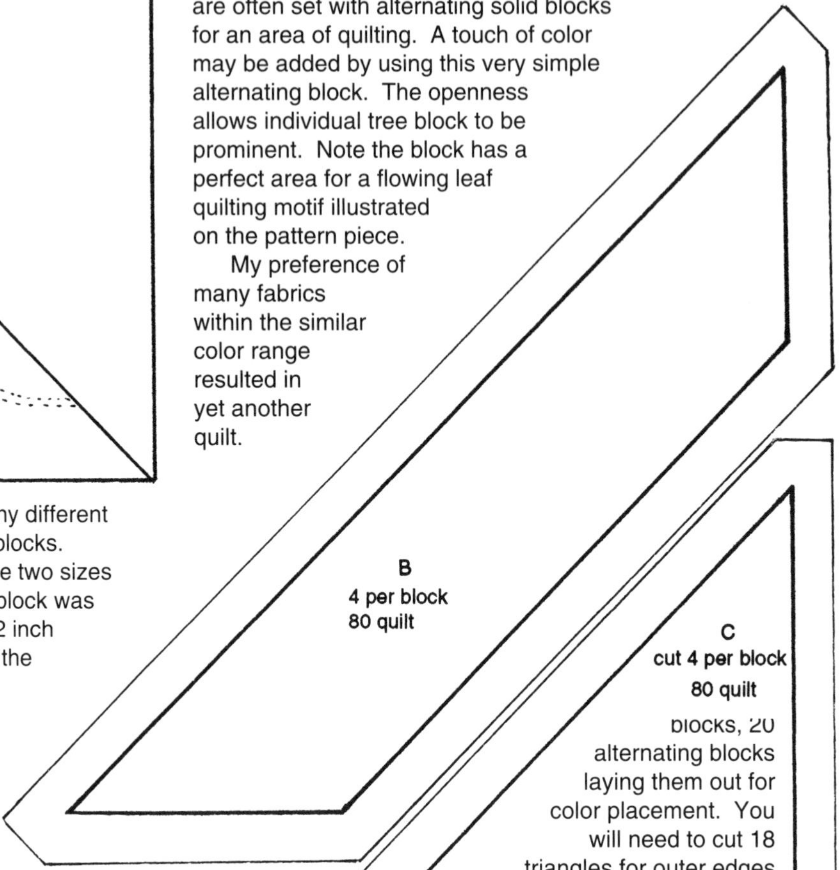

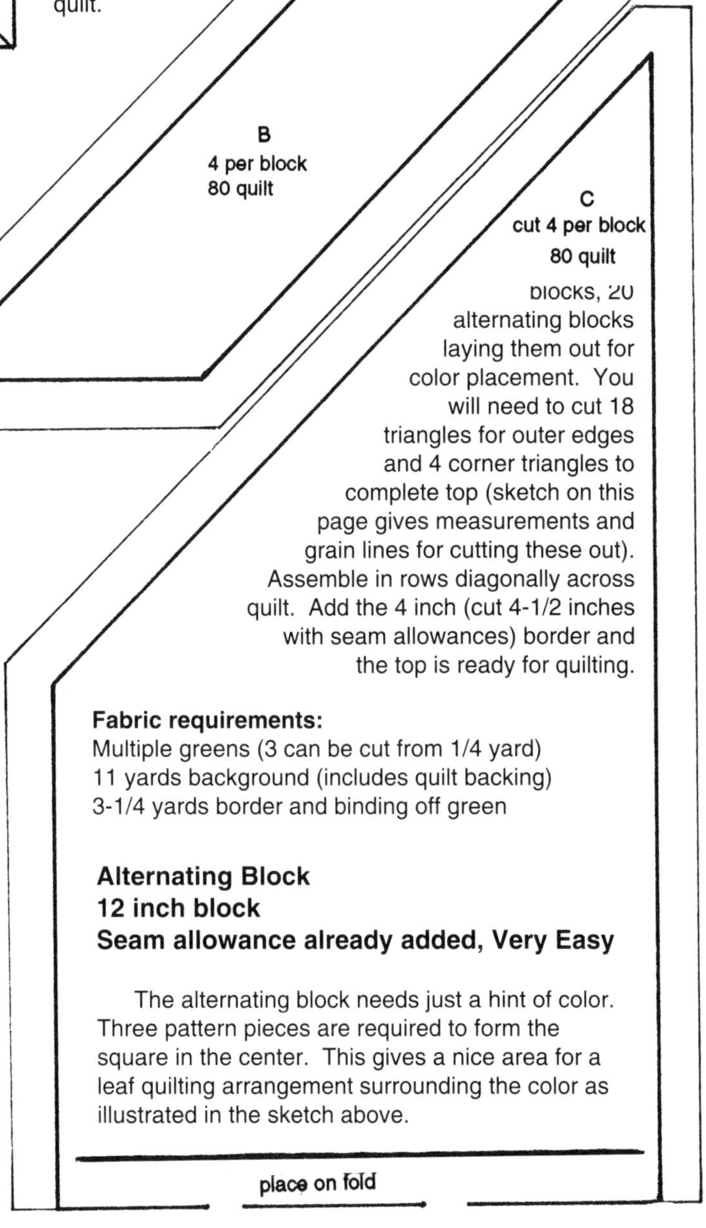

A

B

C

leaf quilting detail

blocks, 20 alternating blocks laying them out for color placement. You will need to cut 18 triangles for outer edges and 4 corner triangles to complete top (sketch on this page gives measurements and grain lines for cutting these out). Assemble in rows diagonally across quilt. Add the 4 inch (cut 4-1/2 inches with seam allowances) border and the top is ready for quilting.

B
4 per block
80 quilt

C
cut 4 per block
80 quilt

4 x 110"

12" 12" 17" 12" 8-1/2"

4 x 93"

Fabric requirements:
Multiple greens (3 can be cut from 1/4 yard)
11 yards background (includes quilt backing)
3-1/4 yards border and binding off green

Alternating Block
12 inch block
Seam allowance already added, Very Easy

The alternating block needs just a hint of color. Three pattern pieces are required to form the square in the center. This gives a nice area for a leaf quilting arrangement surrounding the color as illustrated in the sketch above.

place on fold

Pine Tree Block, 8 and 12 inch
Add Seam Allowance

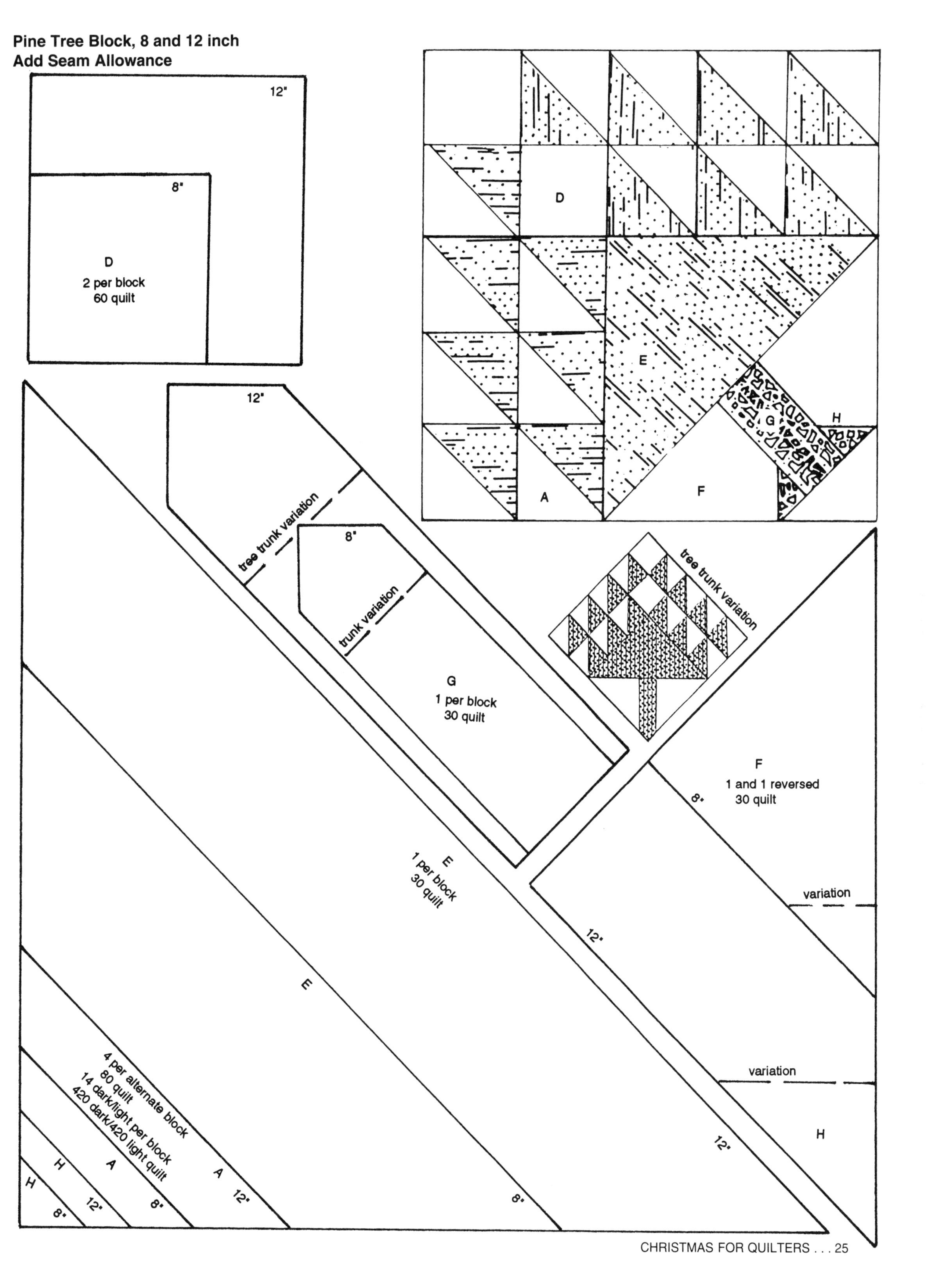

Tall Pine Tree

93 x 99 inches, 12 inch block
Add seam allowance, Easy
Shown in color on page 35

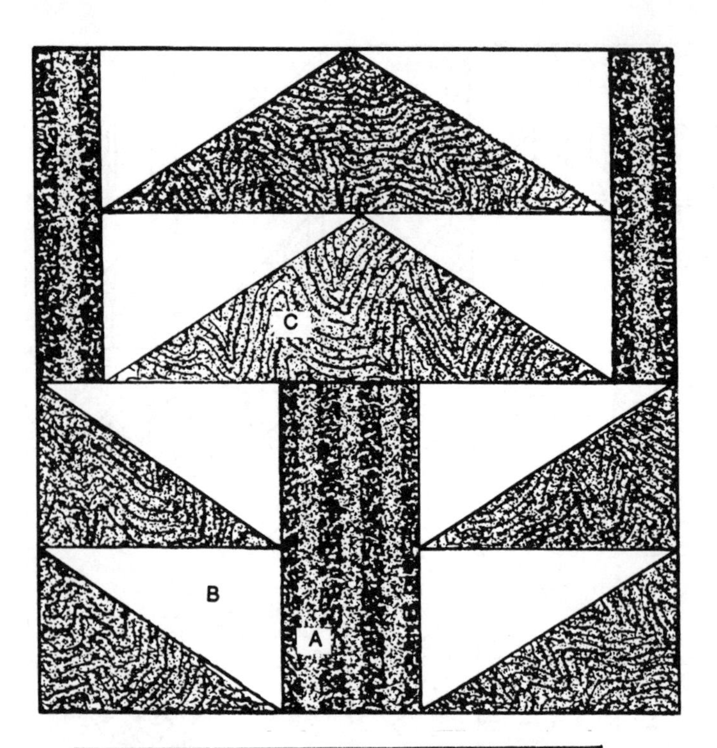

The Tall Pine Tree block makes a forest of interwoven trees using just three pattern pieces. Once together, it is difficult to tell where one block ends and the next begins. Tall Pine Tree is an early documented pattern published in the book, ROMANCE OF THE PATCHWORK QUILT IN AMERICA, Hall and Kretsinger, c1935.

The quilt colors are suggestive of autumn with touches of gold and tan intermingled with the green trees. With fabrics sorted into a green box, a red box, a brown box, a gold box, etc, collecting fabrics was easy. Various greens were cut out for the main trees with a palette of color for the secondary row of trees deep in the forest.

Color adds interest and helps identify the individual trees as well as rows of trees.

You may choose to make your quilt a two-color pine tree by using dark and medium green with your background fabric. This would give a recessed look to the rows that seemed tucked in behind the stronger color trees.

To piece a single block, the trunk of a tree should be half the size of whole trunk shape. Note broken line down middle of pattern below. When piecing the whole quilt, check illustration to see assembly process of partial block rows.

Fabric requirements:

Multiple green prints (can cut 6 per healthy 1/4 yard)

11 yards background (includes back of quilt)

2-7/8 yards border fabric (which includes binding off fabric)

2-7/8 yards inner tan border (unless use 1-1/2 yards which would require piecing border strips)

center for outer edge trunk (add seam allowance to this line)

A

49 full dark green trunks

49 secondary color tree trunks

B

cut 368 background

112 dark trees
84 lighter trees
12 background

C

Christmas Gift Wrap
English Ivy Block

29-1/2 x 38 inch quilt (8 inch block)
Add seam allowance, Medium
Shown in color on page 34

Artists in the gift wrapping paper industry have borrowed from quilt designs for their colorful wrapping paper. It is because of this overlapping of designs that the gift wrap idea for a quilt was drawn out and made. It looks like a big gift that is wrapped in quilt designed paper. A single large 12 inch poinsettia block can be seen in the poinsettia section on page 49.

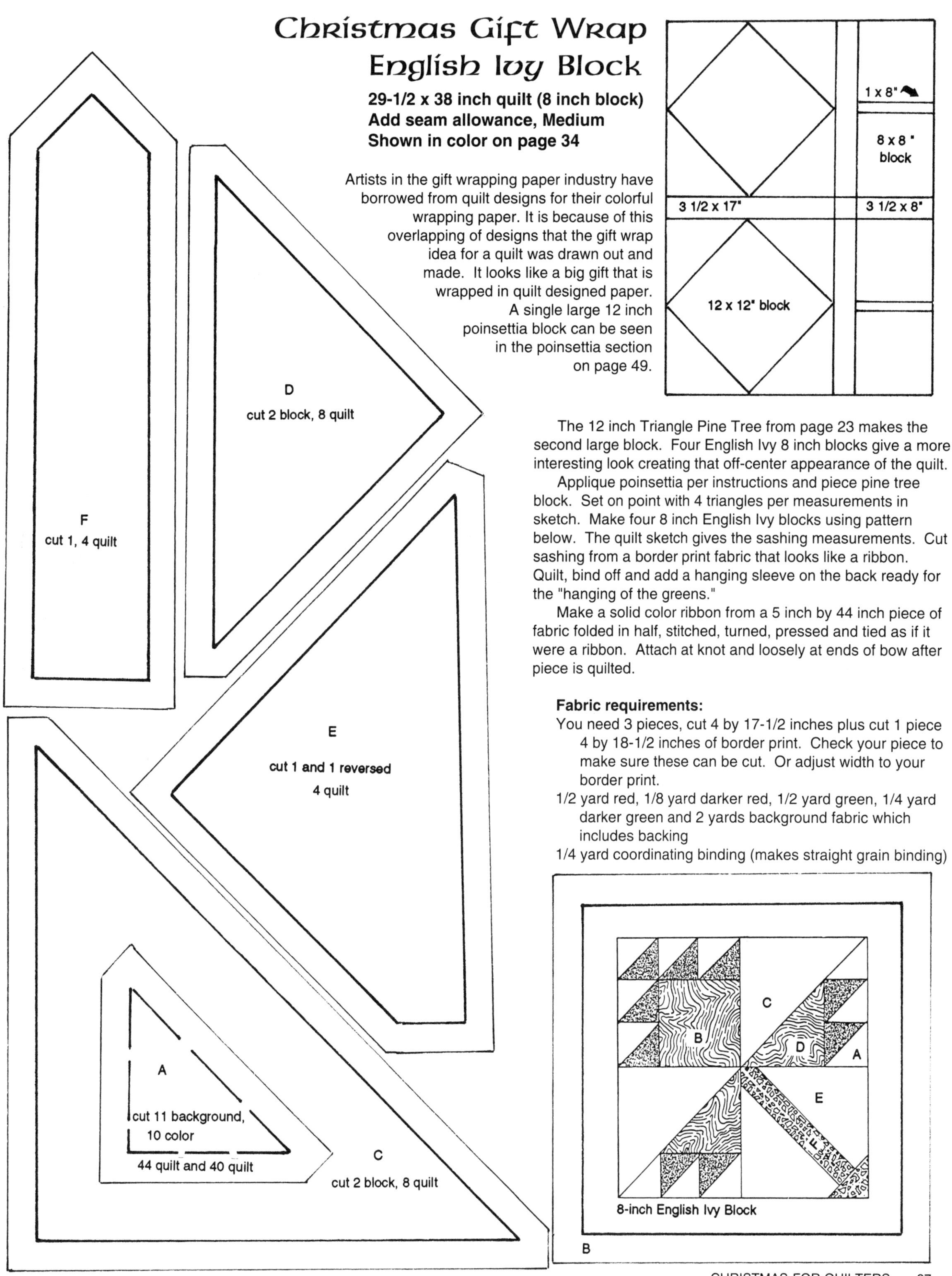

The 12 inch Triangle Pine Tree from page 23 makes the second large block. Four English Ivy 8 inch blocks give a more interesting look creating that off-center appearance of the quilt.

Applique poinsettia per instructions and piece pine tree block. Set on point with 4 triangles per measurements in sketch. Make four 8 inch English Ivy blocks using pattern below. The quilt sketch gives the sashing measurements. Cut sashing from a border print fabric that looks like a ribbon. Quilt, bind off and add a hanging sleeve on the back ready for the "hanging of the greens."

Make a solid color ribbon from a 5 inch by 44 inch piece of fabric folded in half, stitched, turned, pressed and tied as if it were a ribbon. Attach at knot and loosely at ends of bow after piece is quilted.

Fabric requirements:

You need 3 pieces, cut 4 by 17-1/2 inches plus cut 1 piece 4 by 18-1/2 inches of border print. Check your piece to make sure these can be cut. Or adjust width to your border print.

1/2 yard red, 1/8 yard darker red, 1/2 yard green, 1/4 yard darker green and 2 yards background fabric which includes backing

1/4 yard coordinating binding (makes straight grain binding)

8-inch English Ivy Block

Holly Quilt with Poinsettia Star Block

92 x 106 inches, 8 inch block
Add seam allowance, Easy
Shown in color inside front cover

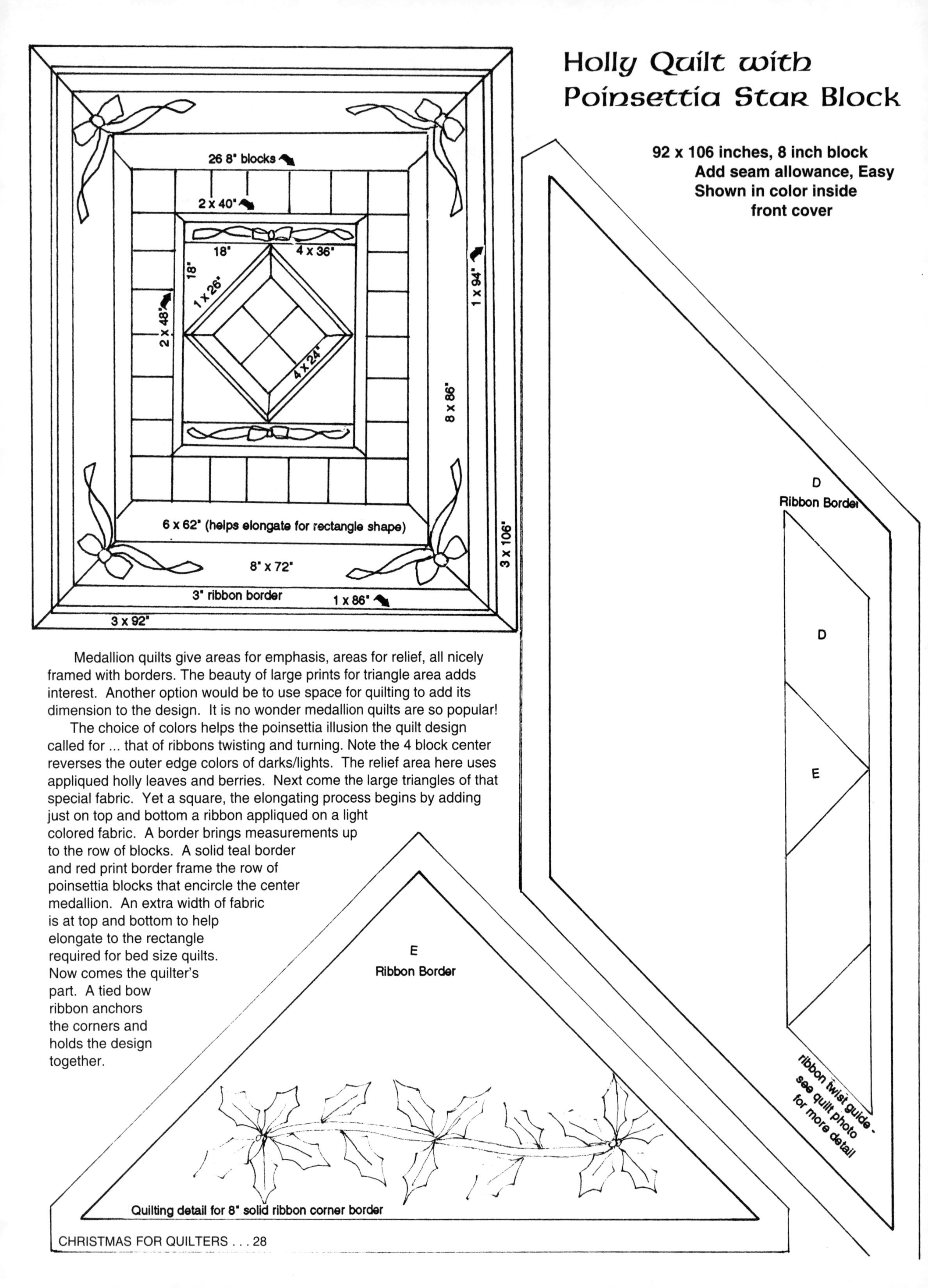

Medallion quilts give areas for emphasis, areas for relief, all nicely framed with borders. The beauty of large prints for triangle area adds interest. Another option would be to use space for quilting to add its dimension to the design. It is no wonder medallion quilts are so popular!

The choice of colors helps the poinsettia illusion the quilt design called for ... that of ribbons twisting and turning. Note the 4 block center reverses the outer edge colors of darks/lights. The relief area here uses appliqued holly leaves and berries. Next come the large triangles of that special fabric. Yet a square, the elongating process begins by adding just on top and bottom a ribbon appliqued on a light colored fabric. A border brings measurements up to the row of blocks. A solid teal border and red print border frame the row of poinsettia blocks that encircle the center medallion. An extra width of fabric is at top and bottom to help elongate to the rectangle required for bed size quilts. Now comes the quilter's part. A tied bow ribbon anchors the corners and holds the design together.

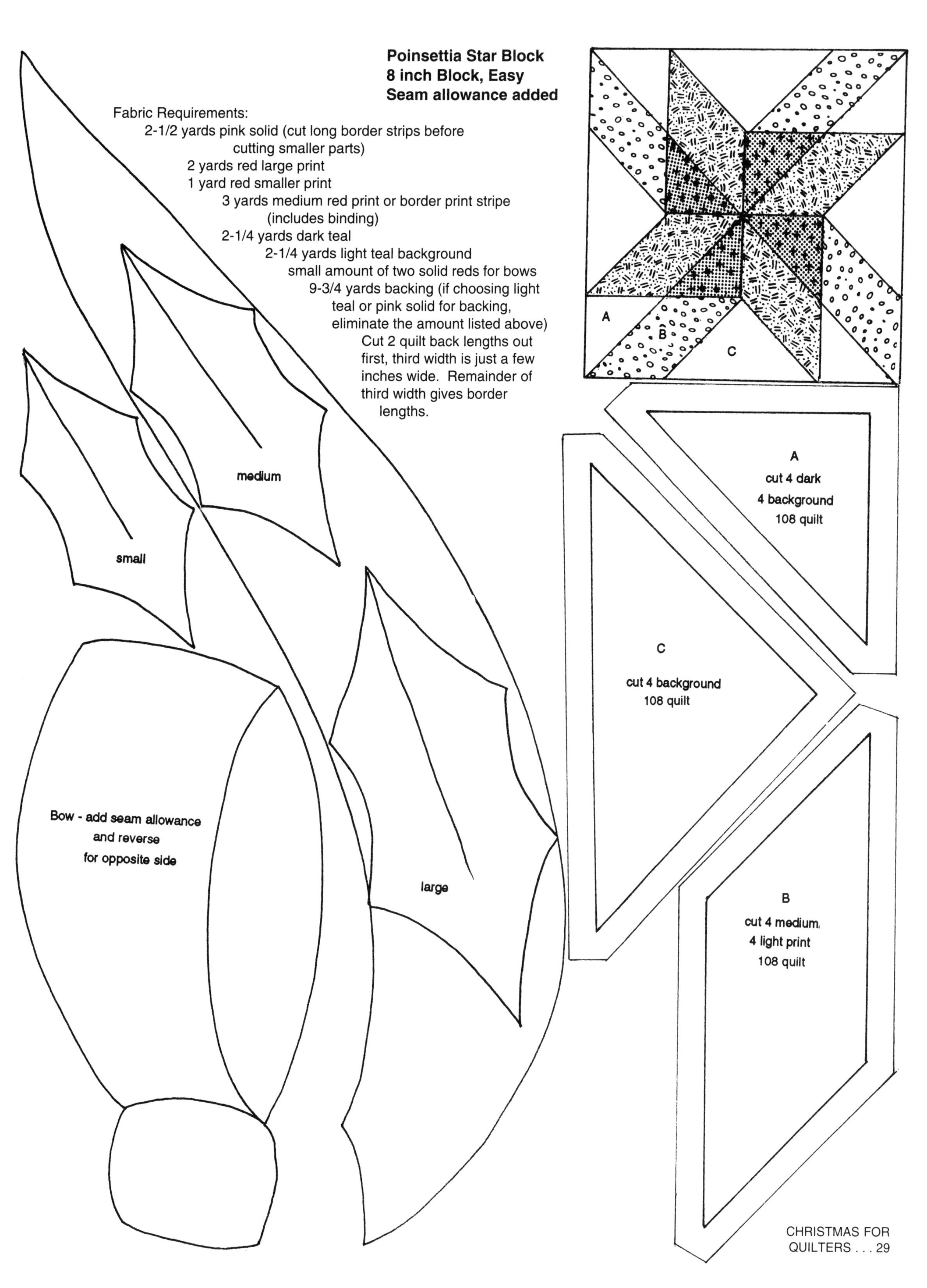

Poinsettia Star Block
8 inch Block, Easy
Seam allowance added

Fabric Requirements:

2-1/2 yards pink solid (cut long border strips before cutting smaller parts)
2 yards red large print
1 yard red smaller print
3 yards medium red print or border print stripe (includes binding)
2-1/4 yards dark teal
2-1/4 yards light teal background
small amount of two solid reds for bows
9-3/4 yards backing (if choosing light teal or pink solid for backing, eliminate the amount listed above)
Cut 2 quilt back lengths out first, third width is just a few inches wide. Remainder of third width gives border lengths.

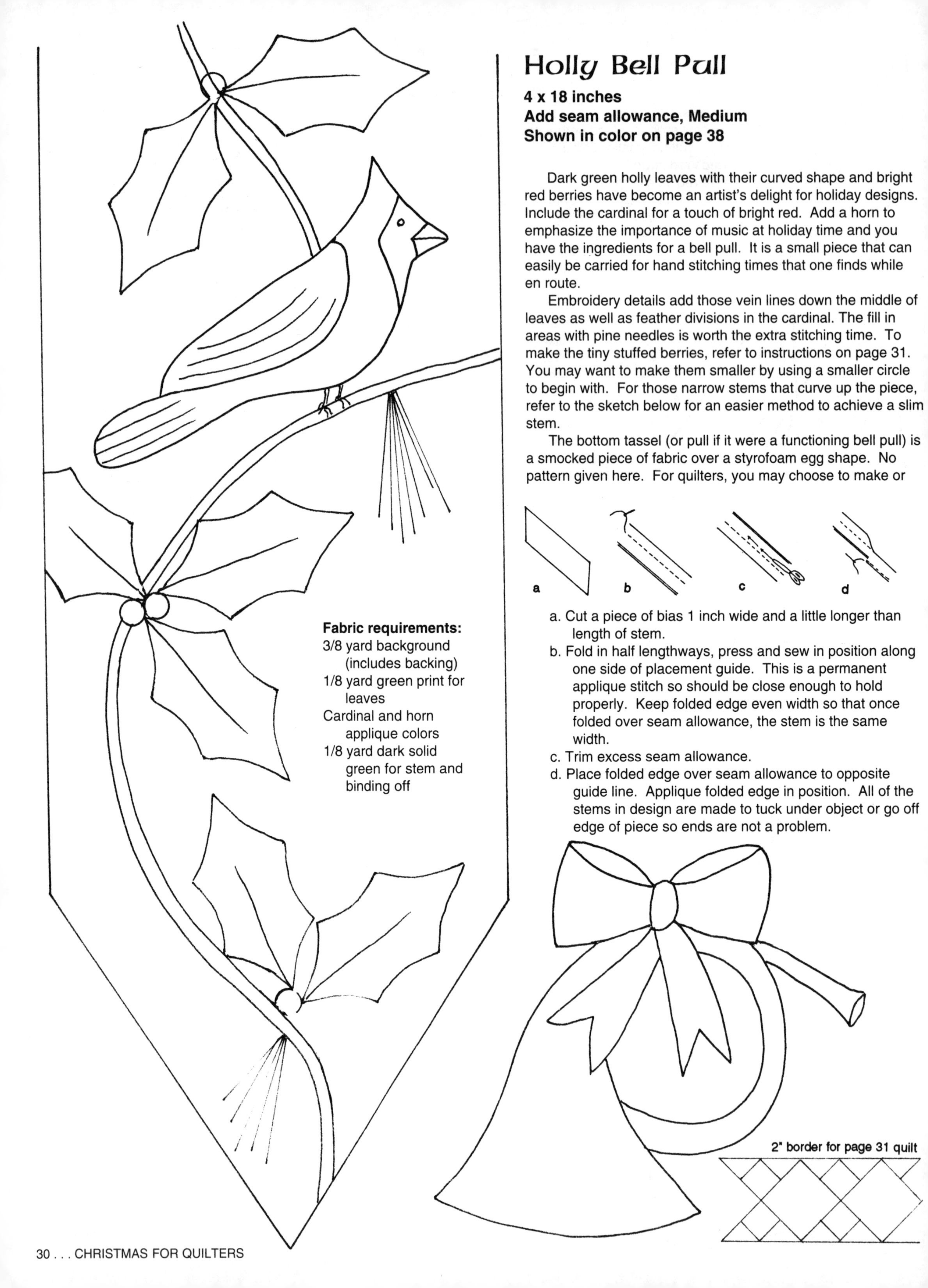

Holly Bell Pull

4 x 18 inches
Add seam allowance, Medium
Shown in color on page 38

Dark green holly leaves with their curved shape and bright red berries have become an artist's delight for holiday designs. Include the cardinal for a touch of bright red. Add a horn to emphasize the importance of music at holiday time and you have the ingredients for a bell pull. It is a small piece that can easily be carried for hand stitching times that one finds while en route.

Embroidery details add those vein lines down the middle of leaves as well as feather divisions in the cardinal. The fill in areas with pine needles is worth the extra stitching time. To make the tiny stuffed berries, refer to instructions on page 31. You may want to make them smaller by using a smaller circle to begin with. For those narrow stems that curve up the piece, refer to the sketch below for an easier method to achieve a slim stem.

The bottom tassel (or pull if it were a functioning bell pull) is a smocked piece of fabric over a styrofoam egg shape. No pattern given here. For quilters, you may choose to make or

a. Cut a piece of bias 1 inch wide and a little longer than length of stem.
b. Fold in half lengthways, press and sew in position along one side of placement guide. This is a permanent applique stitch so should be close enough to hold properly. Keep folded edge even width so that once folded over seam allowance, the stem is the same width.
c. Trim excess seam allowance.
d. Place folded edge over seam allowance to opposite guide line. Applique folded edge in position. All of the stems in design are made to tuck under object or go off edge of piece so ends are not a problem.

Fabric requirements:
3/8 yard background (includes backing)
1/8 yard green print for leaves
Cardinal and horn applique colors
1/8 yard dark solid green for stem and binding off

Holly Heart Wreath

34 x 34 inches,
12 inch block
Add seam allowance,
Medium
Shown in color on
page 33

The dark green color and unusual shape of the holly leaf mixed with the bright red berries make this plant one that many artists use for holiday projects. Quilters often use the flow of a wreath for applique designs.

The Holiday Quilters story is on page 32. As one of the six Holiday Quilters, Linda Gabriesle of Grand Rapids chose the Holly Heart Wreath because of her love of hearts and intricate applique. Embroider the heart line on the background fabric and position the holly leaves and berries per sketch. Add a touch of embroidery in pine needles to fill in some spaces.

The second quilter added the pieced row, while the third quilter added the plaid/gold and triangles to set on point.

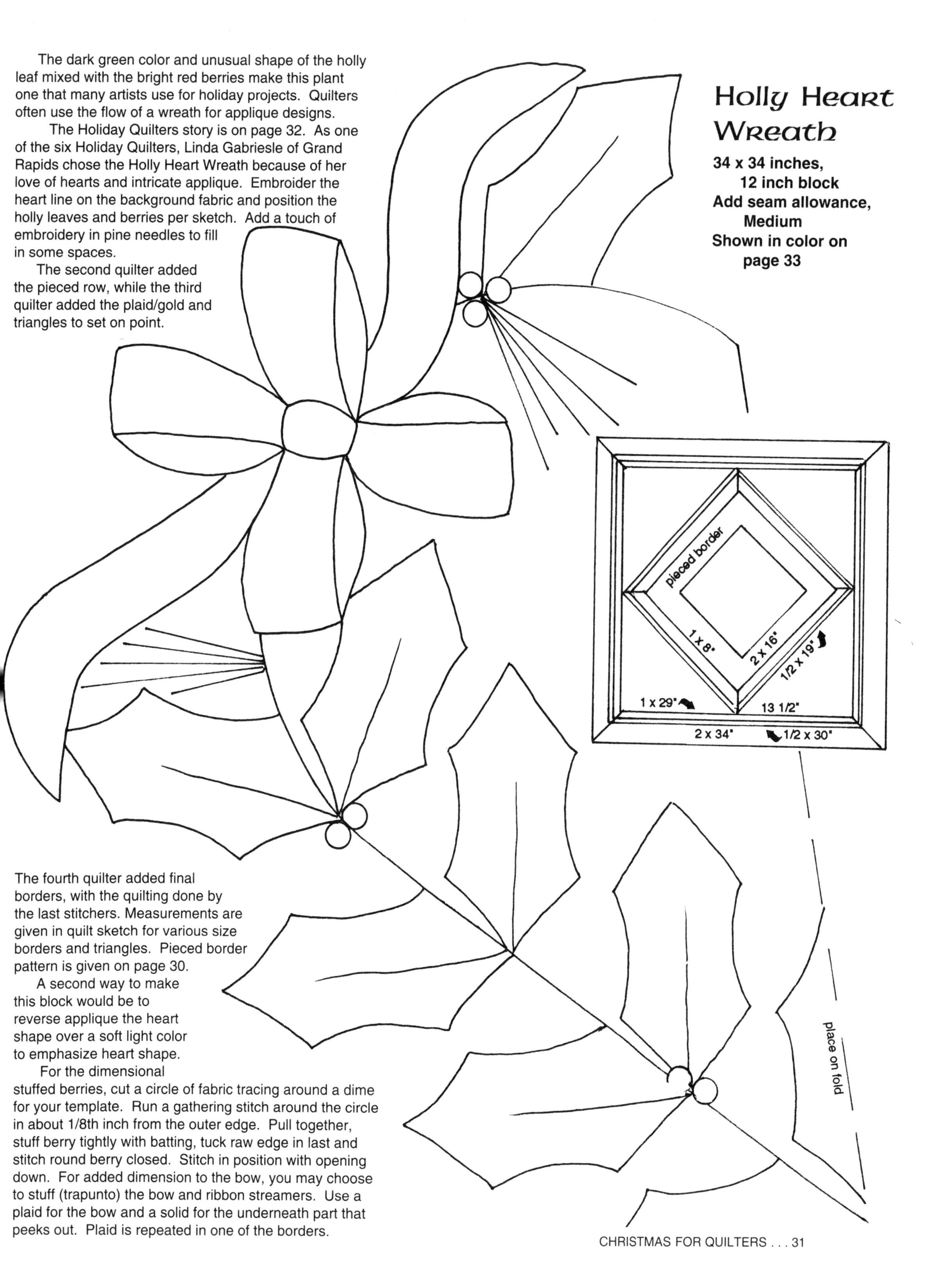

The fourth quilter added final borders, with the quilting done by the last stitchers. Measurements are given in quilt sketch for various size borders and triangles. Pieced border pattern is given on page 30.

A second way to make this block would be to reverse applique the heart shape over a soft light color to emphasize heart shape.

For the dimensional stuffed berries, cut a circle of fabric tracing around a dime for your template. Run a gathering stitch around the circle in about 1/8th inch from the outer edge. Pull together, stuff berry tightly with batting, tuck raw edge in last and stitch round berry closed. Stitch in position with opening down. For added dimension to the bow, you may choose to stuff (trapunto) the bow and ribbon streamers. Use a plaid for the bow and a solid for the underneath part that peeks out. Plaid is repeated in one of the borders.

Holiday Quilters Take on a Creative Challenge

The results of six Michigan quilters' creative challenge can be seen in color on page 33 and inside the back cover. The story of these quilts follows.

While thinking of the January lull approaching after the busy holiday season, I decided to invite several quilting friends from around the west Michigan area to join me in some winter fun. They were selected for their interest in quilting, their distance from each other, and their interest in experimenting with creativity. It is easier to develop an idea and carry it to completion than to pick up on another's project mid-stream. Here is how the creative challenge worked.

We met and established a few ground rules. Each quilter would choose a block from a dozen drawn out for them to choose from. A fabric packet had been prepared for each to use. Once each quilter worked on the piece, it would return to the original block person as her own piece. We met initially and then relied on mail to pass pieces along. We did not discuss them with each other for the most part.

With six participating, we were allowing 3 weeks per move. A specific task assignment was to be accomplished with each move as follows: First meeting - get acquainted, select pattern and fabric packet; Second move - add to block; Third move - add to block (second and third moves could be border, square up, or use your design skills to add to original block); Fourth move - Final border (make sure quilt looks completed); Fifth move - quilting; Sixth move - continue quilting. We decided we did not need more unfinished projects and that quilting was an important design aspect of a project.

I had drawn out a dozen holiday designs for each quilter to choose one as the center block of a wall quilt. Some were pieced, some applique, some very simple, others rather difficult, and a few could become a quilt for any season. The fabrics were gathered from Hoffman California Fabrics where we experimented on those beautiful metallic fabrics. Wonderful plaids from Fasco, designed by Roberta Horton and Leslie Beck, in Christmas colors were added. Those delightful RJR small prints filled in and complemented the metallics and plaids...all working together for best use to achieve the desired effect. Each quilter was given 11 different 1/3 yard pieces with the option of requesting more as long as supplies lasted. Naturally, there were a couple of favorites!

The fabric kit provided gave basic fabrics with the option to add others. No two kits were alike although each fabric was in three of the kits. The fabric packet moved along with each quilt so that the piece would be coordinated from block through whatever happened. Batting and backing were included.

We strived to be prompt with the moving dates established at the first meeting so that each person had a good amount of time without the project dragging on too far into springtime. Naturally a party was called for to see what happened to the quilts as they moved along. The quilts will be hung at local guild quilt shows for all to see.

C

cut 24 dark/24 light sawtooth

B
A
C
D
16"
11 1/2"
11 1/2"
1/2 x 32"
3 x 38"

Nine Patch Holly Quilt
38 x 38 inches
Add seam allowance
Shown in color on inside back cover

For the complete story of this quilt's beginning, read the story of six Holiday Quilters above. Milly Splitstone from Fremont, Michigan chose the nine patch quilt block for her beginning. The nine patch was made by adding applique holly leaves before sending it to the second quilter. She added the border triangles using the same background which gives the appearance that these triangles are part of the original block and are done in a sawtooth pattern. The third quilter added the black triangles with a touch of applique carrying out the holly leaf theme with a bow ribbon. The fourth quilter added triangles/squares to again square the piece up. Two final borders were added to finish off the piece.

Use the pattern piece which includes holly leaf placement. Follow the measurements in the quilt sketch to assemble your quilt.

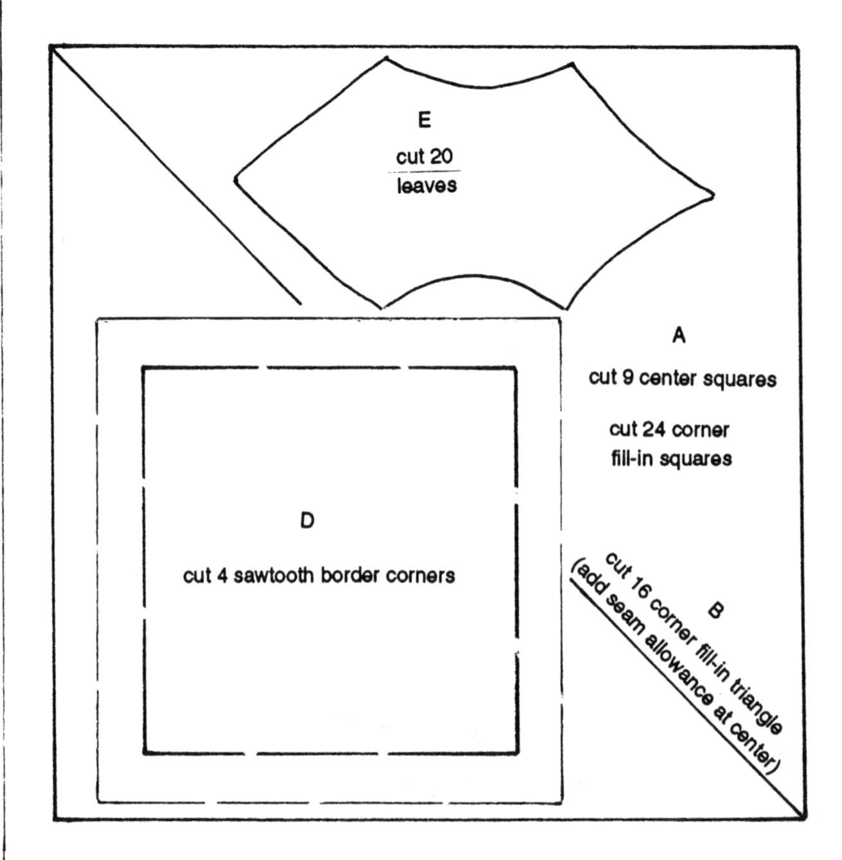

Top Left: Holly Wreath, pages 31, 32.
Bottom Left: Santa in Sleigh, pages 18, 32
Top Right: Church, pages 4, 32
Bottom Right: The Stockings Were Hung, pages 32, 42

Hexagon Wreath, page 48

Hexagon Tree, page 48

Gift Wrapping Paper Quilt, page 27

Christmas Tree Quilt with Star Ornaments, pages 68-70

Pine Tree, pages 24-25

Tall Pine Tree, page 26

Shadows in Forest Quilt using Forest Pine block, pages 19-22

Twelve Days of Christmas, pages 59-64

Holiday Stockings, pages 43-46

Cone Ornament, page 3

Barb

Holiday Sampler, page 65

Holly Bell Pull, page 30

Forest Pine Table Runner, page 22

Mailbox, page 72

Star Tablecover and/or Tree Skirt, page 56

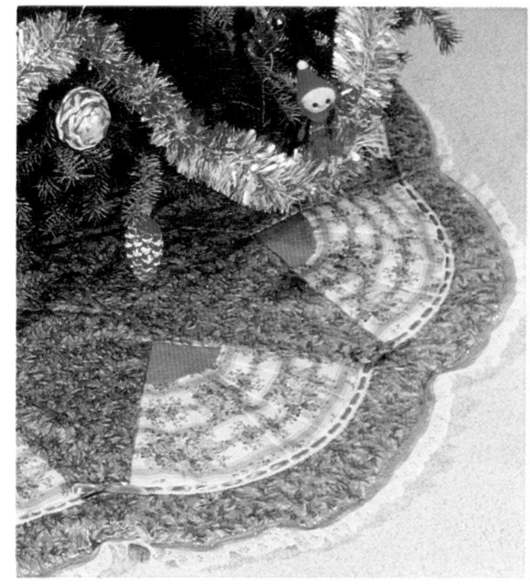

Top Left: Ribbon Tree Skirt, page 58
Middle Left: Rosalia Flower Garden/ Jack's Chain Tree Skirt, page 55
Bottom Left: Triangle Tree Skirt, page 54
Top and Bottom Right: Fan Tree Skirt, page 57
Middle Right: Star Tree Skirt, page 56
Dove Ornament, page 64

Three Wisemen by Judy Pierce, Virgin Islands, page 41

Cookie Cutter Quilt by Marge Etter, Wisconsin, page 41

I'm Not Even Sleepy by Gail Hunt, Canada, page 41

Creativity with our Guest Artists

Shown in color on page 40

As I travel around the country teaching, lecturing and vending at the booth in a merchant's mall, certain quilts stand out to me that fit the theme of the subject that is uppermost on my mind. And of course, it is the subject of the book currently be planned in my head, or the one that is on the drawing board, while samples are being made for the current project. The three unusual quilts featured here are original designs by the quilt artists. Since they are original designs, actual patterns are not given. They are for your inspiration and enjoyment of quilt making.

The quilt, and the quilter, like many other folk art forms have a lot of nostalgia connected with them. There is probably no greater time than the holiday season to enjoy a wealth of designs and to express the love of giving of one's artistic talent. Shall we explore the creative process through these three quilters.

The Cookie Cutter Quilt, by Marge Etter, 84 x 87 inches

Marge, from Wisconsin, has made three very special quilts for her three daughters. One was a double Irish Chain heavily quilted with antique toys, teddy bears, blocks and pine branches. Another one was a windblown tulip variation. The third one of the holiday quilts is the Cookie Cutter quilt, which has recieved many awards as it has been shown at quilt shows around the country. It took about a year and half to "compose and gather fabrics," three months to construct and another three months to quilt.

Marge used the memory of baking Christmas cookies with her Grandmother and began to collect antique cookie cutters for her patterns. The shapes were needle turned hand applique, and embroidered pine needles were done with two strands of green floss to add filler. She chose a background that reminds her of the color of sugar cookie dough.

A Christmas tree center medallion of cookie cutter shapes, holly leaves, pine cones and embroidery work is bordered by an intricately pieced oval frame. The corners around the oval are filled with a spray of cookie cutter shapes, framed with another pieced border set between two borderprint strips of fabric. A wide area enlarges the quilt to full bed size again having corners filled with designs as it moves outward from the central focal point. Radiating straight quilting lines beautifully enhances the design.

Christmas 1992 was a very special time for Marge and her three daughters as that is the year they received their quilts. "Quilting is a super way to create heirlooms... to pass on a legacy, to share something of our past. Sharing is one of the very best parts."

I'm Not Even Sleepy (Waiting Panes), by Gail Hunt, 50 x 58 inches

Gail is from British Columbia, Canada. There are two names for the quilt. The first was listed with the quilt as it was shown. Somewhere along the route from her home through a quilt shop to the Houston Quilt Festival, her title of "Waiting Panes" became separated from the quilt. The quilt was a winner in the Labor of Love competition, sponsored by Wineberry Fabrics quilt shop.

Images of her two youngest children clad in pajamas, peer with excitement out into the Christmas evening sky. Are they waiting for a glimpse of Santa's sleigh? Or are they just too excited to lay their head on a pillow?

Gail had a problem finding just the right sheer cotton fabric to dye to create that light aura of the electric lights around the window. The quilt design was drawn out to its full size so that it could be pieced. The window lights, stained glass at top of window, boughs of holly and the children were appliqued. Quilted mainly in the ditch to emphasize the design, open areas of the side borders feature tree branches. When one looks closer, Santa and a reindeer are quilted in the night sky.

She pieced and appliqued the whole top during two idyllic weeks at a beach cottage in the summer. Quilting took longer! As a sentimentalist, her quilts are strong emotional statements. As Gail says, "Christmas time provides a subject filled with traditions and emotions."

Three Wisemen, "Royalty in Search of a King," by Judy Pierce, 25 x 38 inches

Judy made this wall quilt as an entry in the 1992 Hoffman Challenge, a national challenge to be creative using a selected Hoffman California Fabric. As the challenge fabric deadline loomed, thoughts had already turned to holiday projects. Judy, who resides in the Virgin Islands, drew out the design from memories of bulletin board displays she put together as a Church school superintendent years ago. She once did a similar composition as a stained glass window using colored cellephane with black electrician's tape for the "leading." The drawing featuring the Wisemen as if standing in an archway of an ancient temple was retrived from pattern files.

The challenge fabric took on a more Byzantine look as it lay in the "to-do" box. Bright colors mixed with gold became tiny mosaic tiles to be placed together into a pattern depicting a Biblical event. That is when the majesty and pageantry of the Wisemen coming to Bethlehem came to mind. Because of a St. Croix event...the Three Kings' Day Parade, the piece would not only satisify the urge to do something Christmas-y, but would have an island connotation.

Originally planned to be done as a mosaic using 1 inch squres, the plans changed when the squares seemed to spoil the effect of a broad sky and flowing gowns. The curved angular shapes suited the theme better.

Judy has entered the Hoffman Challenge several times, enjoying the challenge of creating a piece that reflects something of the island flavor.

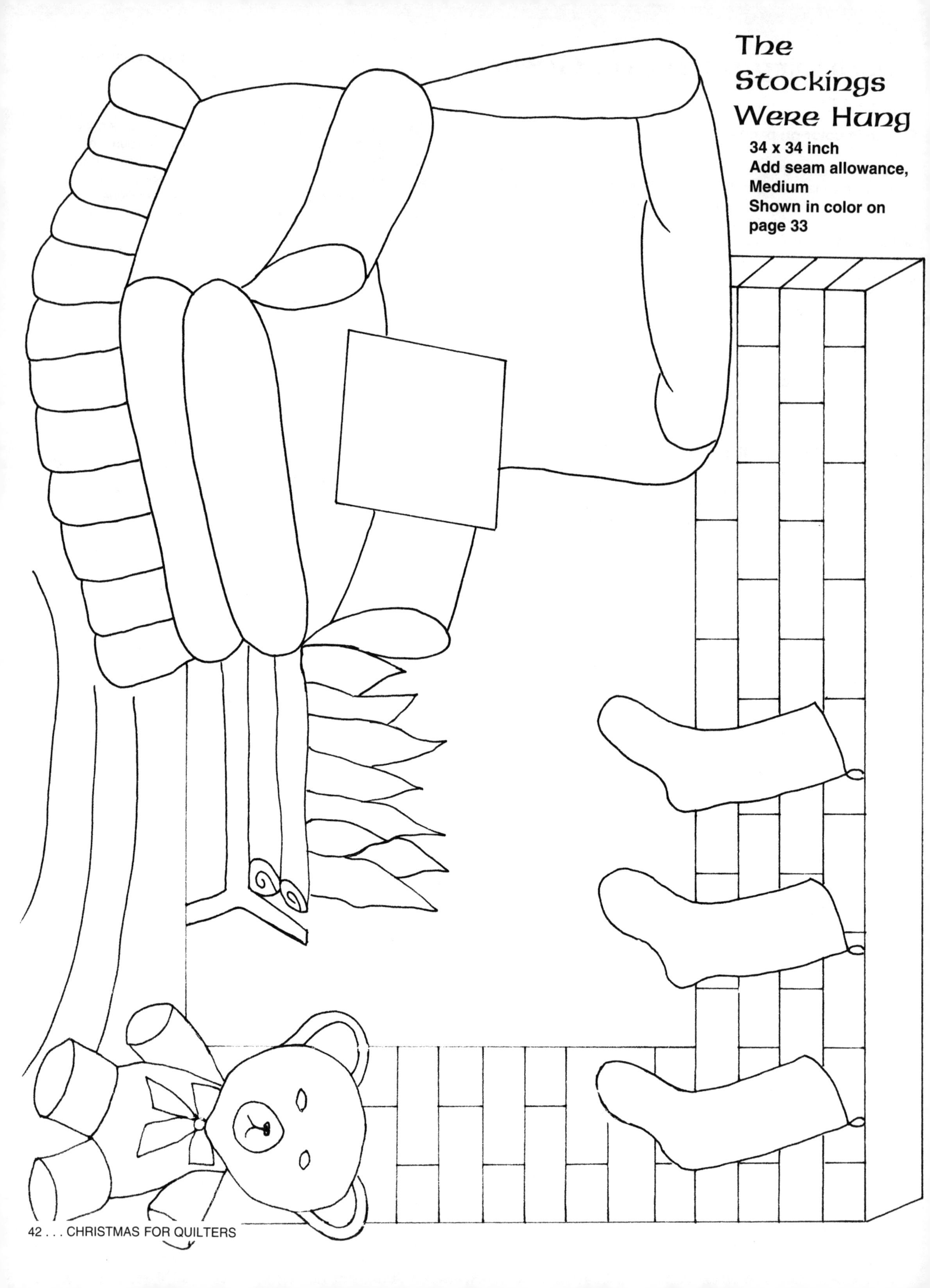

The Stockings Were Hung

34 x 34 inch
Add seam allowance,
Medium
Shown in color on page 33

Stocking Designs Shown in color on

A

B

C

D

D

E

Description from page 42

Starting with a 12 inch block design, Sue Nichols of Muskegon began to make a holiday wall hanging. The story of six Michigan quilters that went on a creative challenge is on page 32. This is one of the quilts made.

Sue loves applique so she chose a design that fit her interest. Using the plaid fabric lines, she was able to achieve a realistic chair. Further dimensions were achieved by moving the chair out from the wall with a dark hearth. The print fabric appears as a rug for the chair and bear to sit on.

I received Sue's scene and needed to add a border to enhance the room, or properly frame it. The idea of a curtain came to mind. Fabric was gathered for side curtains, a valance was pleated for top border. Plain fabric, even one with a floor design didn't seem to work with the folds and pleats on three sides. Crinkling up some fabric, a technique explored by Linda McGehee, solved the problem. The next quilters added borders and appliqued holly leaves to finish off design.

Stockings
Add seam allowance

Stockings can reflect the holiday theme or can be a way to express one's interest or hobbies. They are often done in the reds and greens of the Christmas colors, but why not make them color coordinate with the setting. Unlike quilts, stockings can be made with more elegant fabrics. We feature a chintz and lace stocking lined with satin, a tapestry look, velvet crazy patch, along with the more traditional pieced or appliqued ones. The following are basic step by step instructions for making a stocking.

To Make a Stocking

I. Choose a design style that best fits the person the stocking is for, or the location to be hung.

2. Using the suggested shapes included on these four pages, make the shape on paper, remembering that you will need to add seam allowance as you cut out the shapes.

3. Prepare stocking front... piece, applique or cut shape of stocking. Decide whether quilting is required. If not, add a light weight interfacing to give body to the stocking. Once the front is finished, make a back the same size. Quilt or interface the back as well. Stitch front to back.

4. Cut 2 lining shapes just 1/4 inch smaller, tapering to exact size at top where stocking and lining will be sewn together.

5. With right sides together, sew two lining shapes together leaving a turning hole down in the toe area about 3 inches long. Do not turn.

6. Make a hanging tab and pin in position on the stocking. For full size stocking, cut a piece of coordinating fabric 2-1/2 wide by 6 inches long. Medium size, cut 1-3/4 by 4 inches; for ornament or miniature, cut 1-1/2 by 3 inches. Fold in 1/4th on each side and fold together. Top stitch down each outer edge. Pin in position.

7. Put lining up over stocking until top edges match. Stitch completely around top of stocking. Turn out through turning hole, and stitch closed.

8. Top stitch down 1/4 inch from top edge to hold lining in position.

Stocking Specifics:

A. Basic stocking has the toe/heel shape on page 45 with instructions to continue from given line up 12 inches for a finished 18 inch stocking.

B. Medium size stocking is 9 inches tall and yet wide enough to hold stocking stuffers, design pattern is given on page 46. Ideal for Baby's First Christmas.

C. A 5-1/2 inch miniature tree stocking shape is on page 46. A "Quilter's Stocking" is filled with fat quarters of fabric. To make fat quarter fillers, cut 5 by 5 inch squares to roll up for miniature fat quarters of fabric. For avid quilter, use medium size stocking and fill with actual fat quarters.

D. Sunbonnet Stockings. Cut stocking shape desired. Applique design, add lace or trims and embroider the fine details.

E. Crazy Patch. Prepare crazy patch over muslin foundation before cutting stocking shape.

F. Hearts were appliqued down basic stocking using two different designs. One design features ribbons and the other features a row of hearts. Heart shape on page 44.

G. Strip pieced stocking is prepared over a base shape by sewing various width strips.

H. Patchwork stocking of squares uses many holiday fabrics in 1 or 1-1/2 inch squares.

I. Angled curve top stocking uses boot shape except to round out the toe. A chintz fabric was used with a satin coordinating banding (top band shape given on page 46). Stocking could hang straight out from wall emphasing unusual top shape.

J. Boot shape is on page 45. Add 1 inch by 7 inches wide trim before adding the top shape (illustrated on page 45). Tapestry fabric was used with satin trim and lining. Heel shape is stuffed and sealed off on outer boot. A crochet lace flower with button center was used for trim.

Fabric Requirements:

Large Stocking - 5/8 yard fabric will make 2 stockings, 5/8 yard lining, batting/backing or interfacing, and trims. Medium Stocking - 3/8 yard fabric will make 4 medium size stockings, 3/8 yard lining, batting/backing or interfacing, and trims. Miniature or Ornament Stockings - 1/4 yard fabric will make 6 miniature stockings, 1/4 yard lining, batting/backing or interfacing, and trims. Notes: 1/2 yard of 3 color ribbons were used on heart stockings. 3/4 yard lace gives 2 rows top, heel and toe. 3/8 yard lace gives 1 row top and toe.

F

F

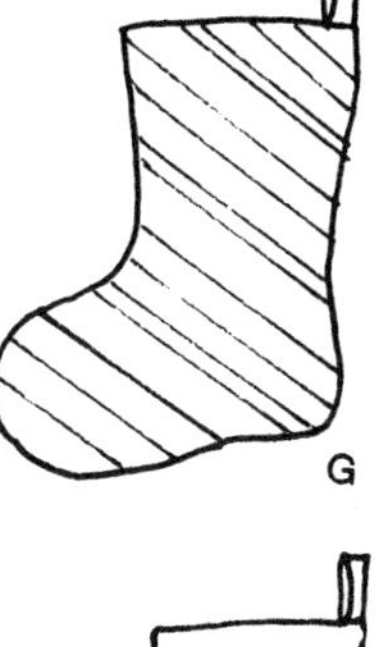
G

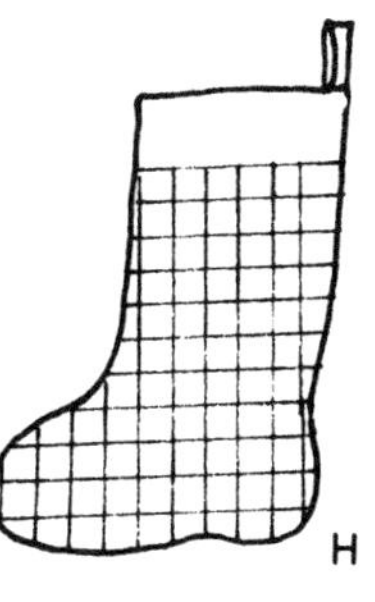
H

I

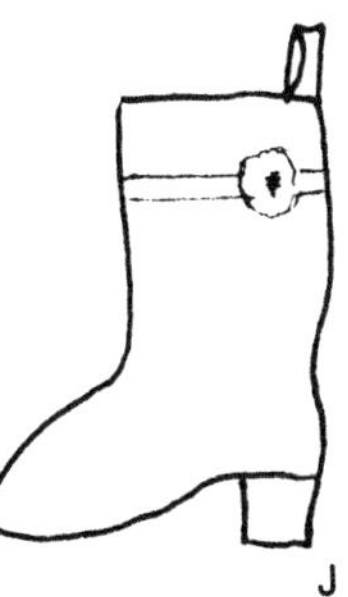
J

The Designs Are Endless...

Basic Stocking

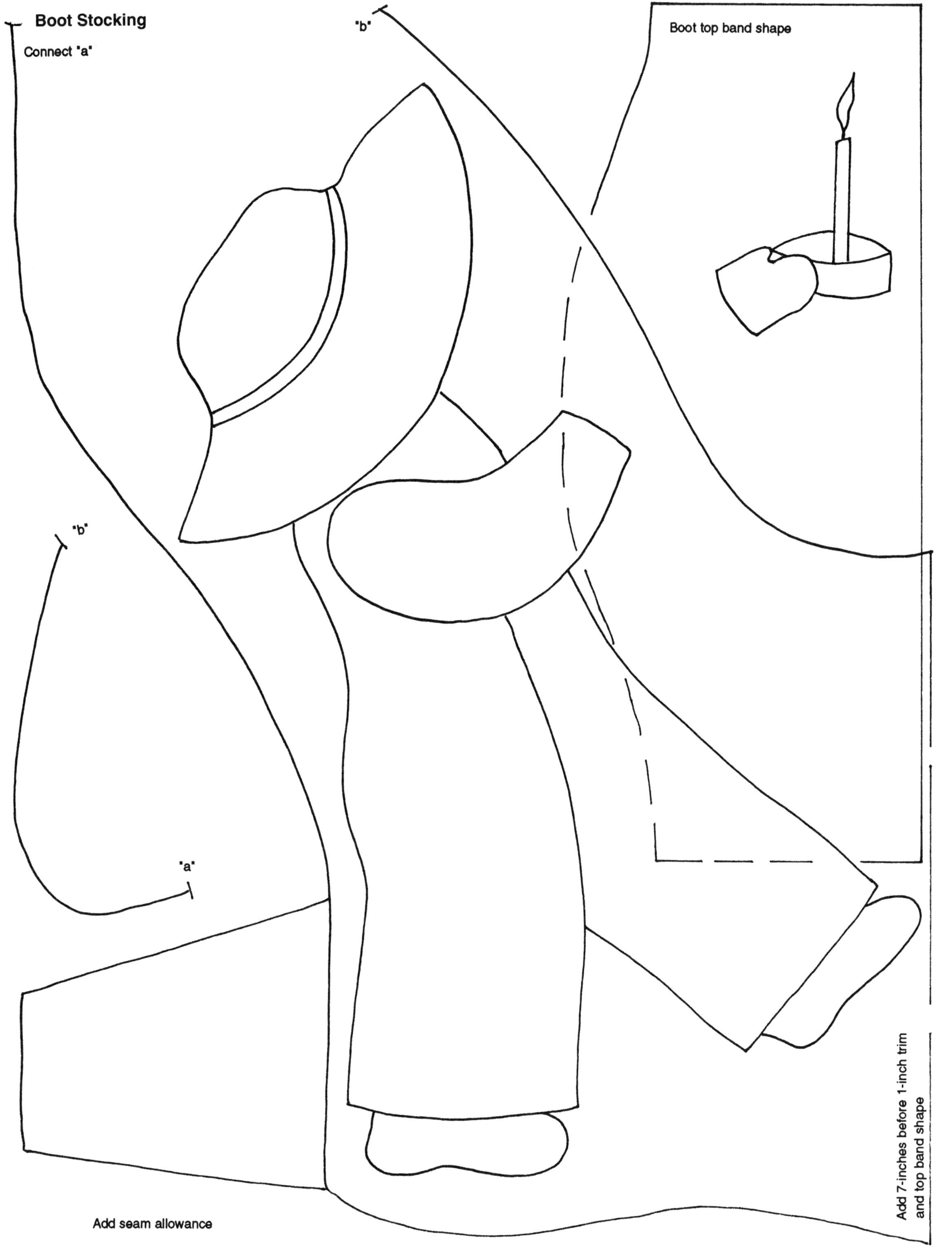
Boot Stocking
Connect "a"
"b"
Boot top band shape
"b"
"a"
Add seam allowance
Add 7-inches before 1-inch trim
and top band shape

Medium and Miniature Stockings
Shape of Curved Top Stocking ("I" on page 43)
Add seam allowance

Drunkard's Path

78 x 90 inches using 3 inch size
104 x 120 inches using 4 inch size
Add seam allowance, Difficult
Shown in color on page 36

One of the blocks handed down from an integral part of our quilt heritage is the two patch curved design. The block with a curved chunk taken out of one corner has different names which depend on the way the curve twists, turns, encircles, hangs from a corner or moves across a quilt in a specific direction. Our holiday red and green quilt is probably the most common setting for these shapes.

Various research sources refer to this setting as Drunkard's Path, Drunkard's Trail, Robbing Peter to Pay Paul, Endless Trail, Old Maid's Puzzle, Solomon's Puzzle, Crooked Path, Wonder of the World, Rocky Road to (you may pick a destination), and the list goes on. None of the names indicate the holidays, so we probably should rename our quilt to a more festive title. I purchased this quilt top while traveling in Texas, so can only guess at the original designer's ideas.

Betty Boyink Publishing has produced a plastic curve template set that includes the Drunkard's Path. If interested, write for detailed information. The patterns below include both the 3 and 4 inch sizes which would produce quilts the size listed above. Use the photograph for a guide.

The block sketched above is 4 across by 4 down or 16 squares of individual drunkard's path. To make the quilt size above, 42 blocks are required. Now doesn't that sound better than to say that 672 individual squares need to be made!

Accuracy is called for, especially with the curve pattern. For best stitching results, clip the "B" curve about four times. By marking the center of both shapes, it is easier to match each end and center for accurately spacing and stitching together. Pin ends, center and extra pin between the pins if needed. Practice helps!

The border width is the same width as block, i.e. 3 inch requires 3 inch border and 4 inch the 4 inch width would be used. Also note that the outermost row of blocks on two sides uses a different green over the darker green of center blocks. This acts as a secondary border before the final red border.

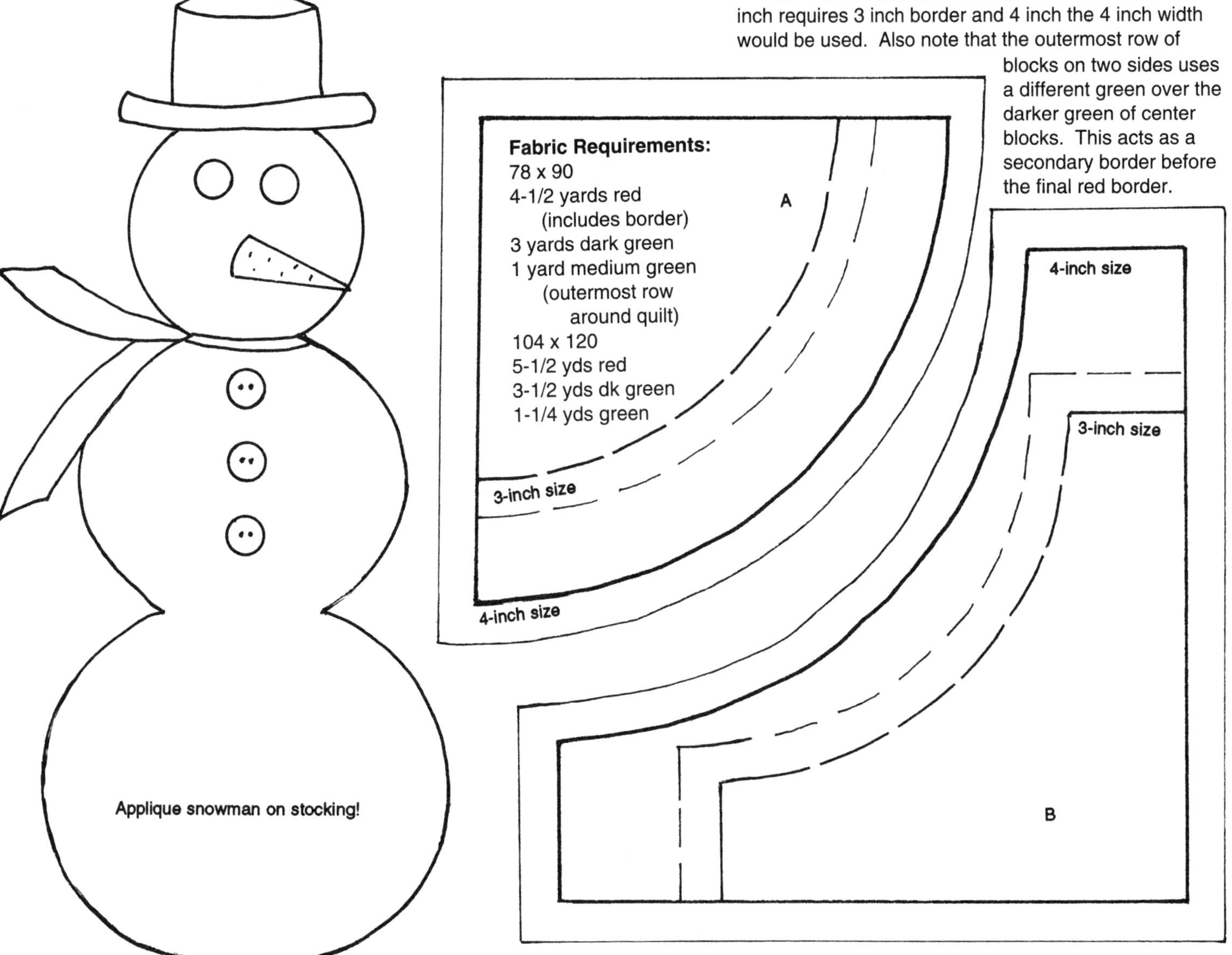

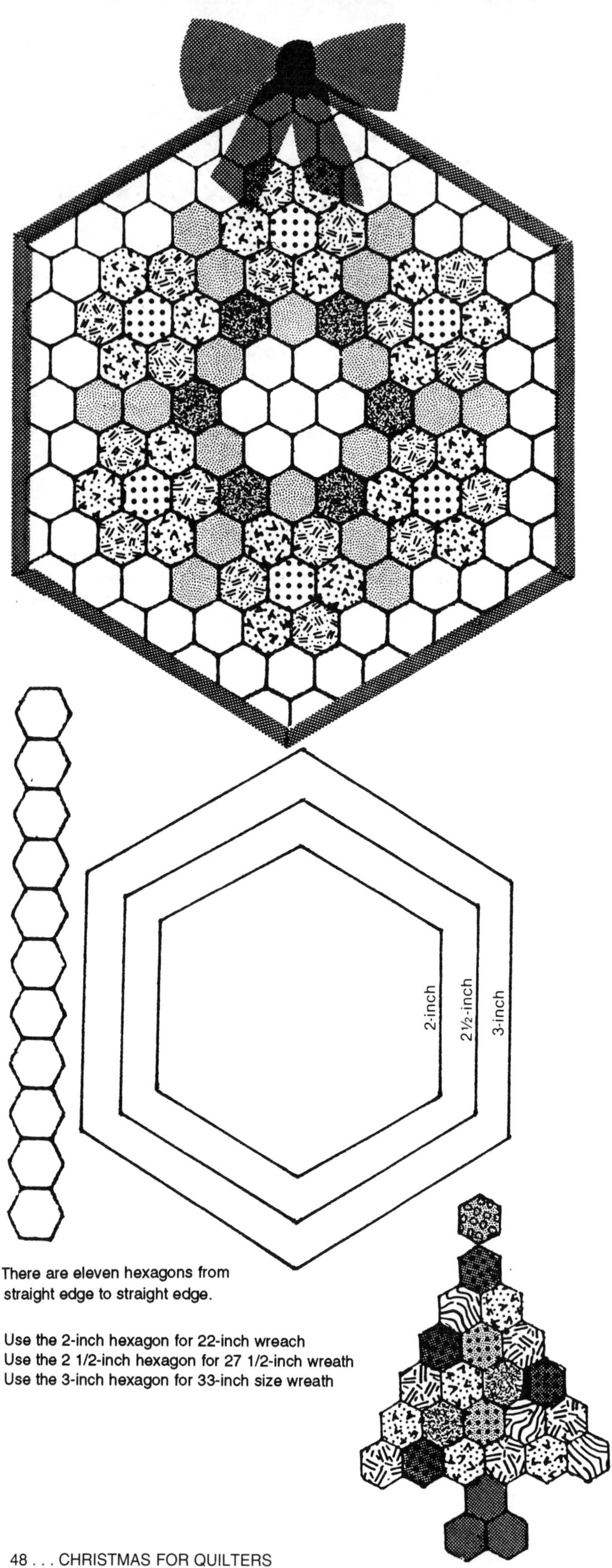

There are eleven hexagons from straight edge to straight edge.

Use the 2-inch hexagon for 22-inch wreach
Use the 2 1/2-inch hexagon for 27 1/2-inch wreath
Use the 3-inch hexagon for 33-inch size wreath

Hexagon Wreath

22, 27 1/2 or 33 inch wreath
Add seam allowance, Medium
Shown in color on page 34

The hexagon shape is often used by quilters for their designs. Here we have a wreath and a tree. Note the pieced Santa on page 16 is based on the hexagon shape. In my home and many other homes, a wreath is one of the first holiday decorations to go up and the last to come down. Some people even leave a wreath up all year round. And why not, festive wreaths are symbols of friendship and hospitality. This wreath uses a single flowerette center of light print background fabric surrounded by 12 hexagons. Six are red prints to simulate holly berries. After the 12 hexagon row, 6 colored flowerettes divided by 2 hexagons round out to make the green wreath. Continue to work to outer edge with background fabric, which brings the piece to the final hexagon shape. Half hexagons are required at outer edges.

Determine the size wreath you would like (measurements are given below patterns). Make your template, adding seam allowance to the hexagon size chosen. Arrange the hexagons in position on a felt board or muslin for ease in moving to sewing machine or favorite chair for hand sewing.

Assemble individual hexagons in rows keeping seam allowance free for ease of fitting next hexagon in position. The result will be one continuous seam as you sew the rows together. This speeds up the process of putting hexagons together.

Quilting can help convey the desired wreath effect. The center 7 hexagons were quilted 1/4 inch inside the seam of each individual hexagon. The wreath portion was quilted in a circular fashion around the center. The bordering hexagons around the perimeter were again quilted 1/4 inch inside the seam. Bind off. Add a red bow made from 5 by 45 inch width of red fabric. Fold in half lengthways, sew raw edges together stitching in a lightweight quilt batting at the same time. A lightly padded bow will stay as fresh as your wreath for as long as it hangs!

Fabric Requirements:
1/4 yard medium green
1/8 yard red
1/8 yard light print
1 yard background (includes backing)
3/8 yard red (bow and binding off)

Hexagon Tree

12 inch block
Add seam allowances, Medium
Shown in color on page 34

Rows of hexagons placed in the shape of a tree would make a wall hanging or a pillow. Piece the hexagons using the photograph as your guide to color placement. Once pieced, applique on background fabric. A ruffle was added by cutting 2 pieces of fabric 5-1/2 by 45 inches. Gather and evenly place fullness around sides of pillow. Add back, stuff and enjoy.

Fabric Requirements:
12 by 16 inch background
25 hexagons
2/3 yard ruffle and back

Poinsettia and Poinsettia Wreath

12 inch blocks
Add seam allowance, Medium
Shown in color on page 34 and inside back cover

The poinsettia is often called the flower of Christmas. Flower, you say? Actually, the poinsettia is the top leaves of the poinsettia plant that turn the dark red color because of the amount of dark versus light that the plant receives. This causes the coloring change as well as a cluster of seeds to develop.

Candles are often an integral part of holiday designs whether Christmas cards, wrapping paper or actual candles used with a plant. Quilters have long used the circular wreath idea for placement of shapes to achieve the design. This poinsettia plant effect features a leaf on either side that reaches out to just touch the next bloom to give that circle flow to the block. With the poinsettia placed in the corners, a perfect spot is left for the candle to be positioned at bottom center. The glow lines could be embroidered or quilting lines.

A

Applique underneath leaves "C" first, then "B" on top, and finish with "A". Remember to add seeds.

C

B

Broken line indicates diagonal placement of design.
Reverse leaf for opposite side.

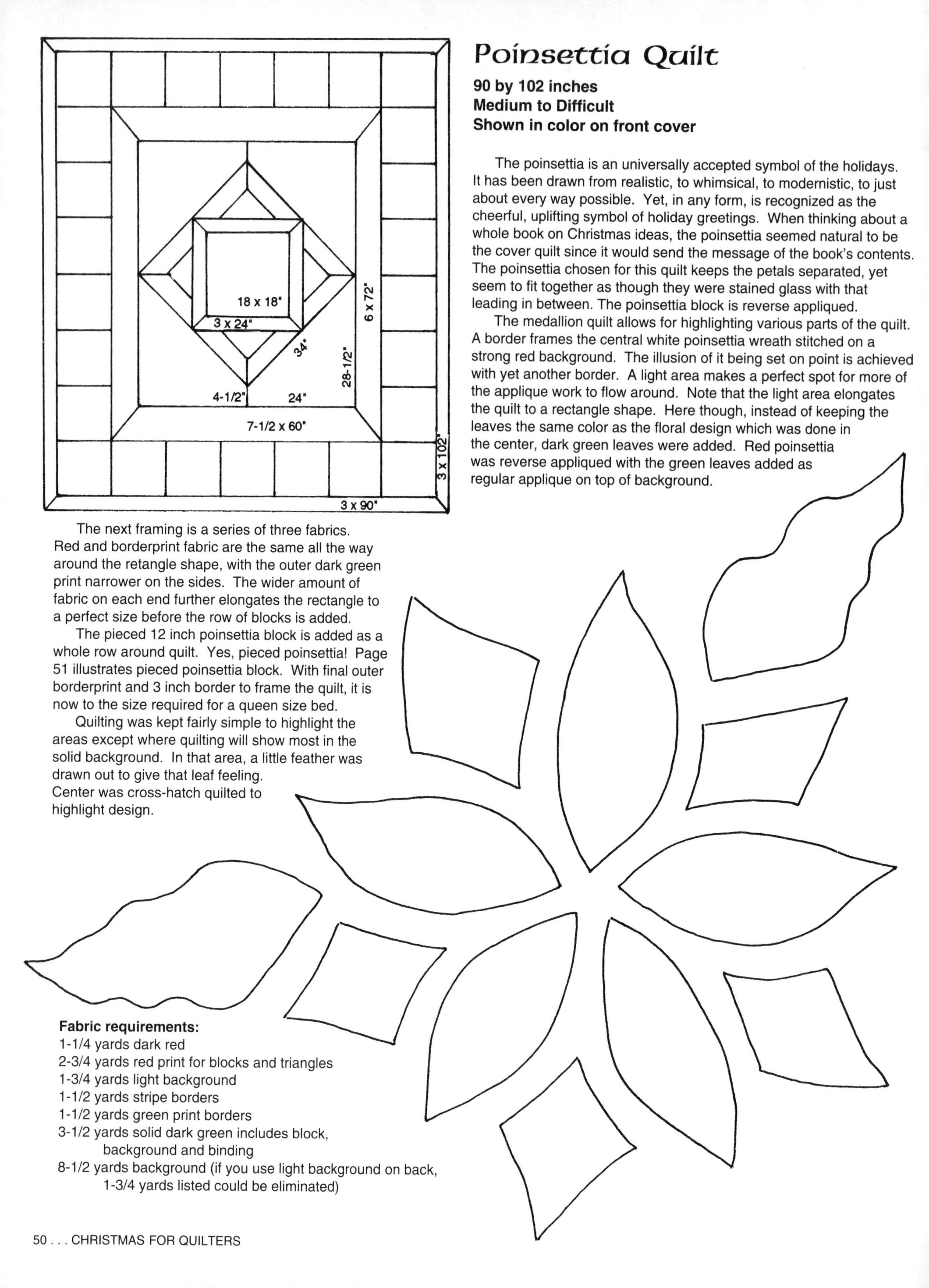

Poinsettia Quilt

90 by 102 inches
Medium to Difficult
Shown in color on front cover

The poinsettia is an universally accepted symbol of the holidays. It has been drawn from realistic, to whimsical, to modernistic, to just about every way possible. Yet, in any form, is recognized as the cheerful, uplifting symbol of holiday greetings. When thinking about a whole book on Christmas ideas, the poinsettia seemed natural to be the cover quilt since it would send the message of the book's contents. The poinsettia chosen for this quilt keeps the petals separated, yet seem to fit together as though they were stained glass with that leading in between. The poinsettia block is reverse appliqued.

The medallion quilt allows for highlighting various parts of the quilt. A border frames the central white poinsettia wreath stitched on a strong red background. The illusion of it being set on point is achieved with yet another border. A light area makes a perfect spot for more of the applique work to flow around. Note that the light area elongates the quilt to a rectangle shape. Here though, instead of keeping the leaves the same color as the floral design which was done in the center, dark green leaves were added. Red poinsettia was reverse appliqued with the green leaves added as regular applique on top of background.

The next framing is a series of three fabrics. Red and borderprint fabric are the same all the way around the retangle shape, with the outer dark green print narrower on the sides. The wider amount of fabric on each end further elongates the rectangle to a perfect size before the row of blocks is added.

The pieced 12 inch poinsettia block is added as a whole row around quilt. Yes, pieced poinsettia! Page 51 illustrates pieced poinsettia block. With final outer borderprint and 3 inch border to frame the quilt, it is now to the size required for a queen size bed.

Quilting was kept fairly simple to highlight the areas except where quilting will show most in the solid background. In that area, a little feather was drawn out to give that leaf feeling.
Center was cross-hatch quilted to highlight design.

Fabric requirements:
1-1/4 yards dark red
2-3/4 yards red print for blocks and triangles
1-3/4 yards light background
1-1/2 yards stripe borders
1-1/2 yards green print borders
3-1/2 yards solid dark green includes block,
background and binding
8-1/2 yards background (if you use light background on back,
1-3/4 yards listed could be eliminated)

Poinsettia Block
12-inch square
Add seam allowance, Difficult

Anytime you have 16 points that come together in the middle, the block does need the "difficult" label for piecing. Could that be why the circle is appliqued over the center? No, it becomes the seed area for the flowering poinsettia! This traditional pattern was available from a mail order pattern company called Aunt Martha, which began in the 1930's.

A word of caution as you begin working with this challenging block. At first glance, it would appear that pattern "A" and "C" are the same size. They are just enough different that care needs to be taken to keep them separated. As you cut, stack and label the two piles.

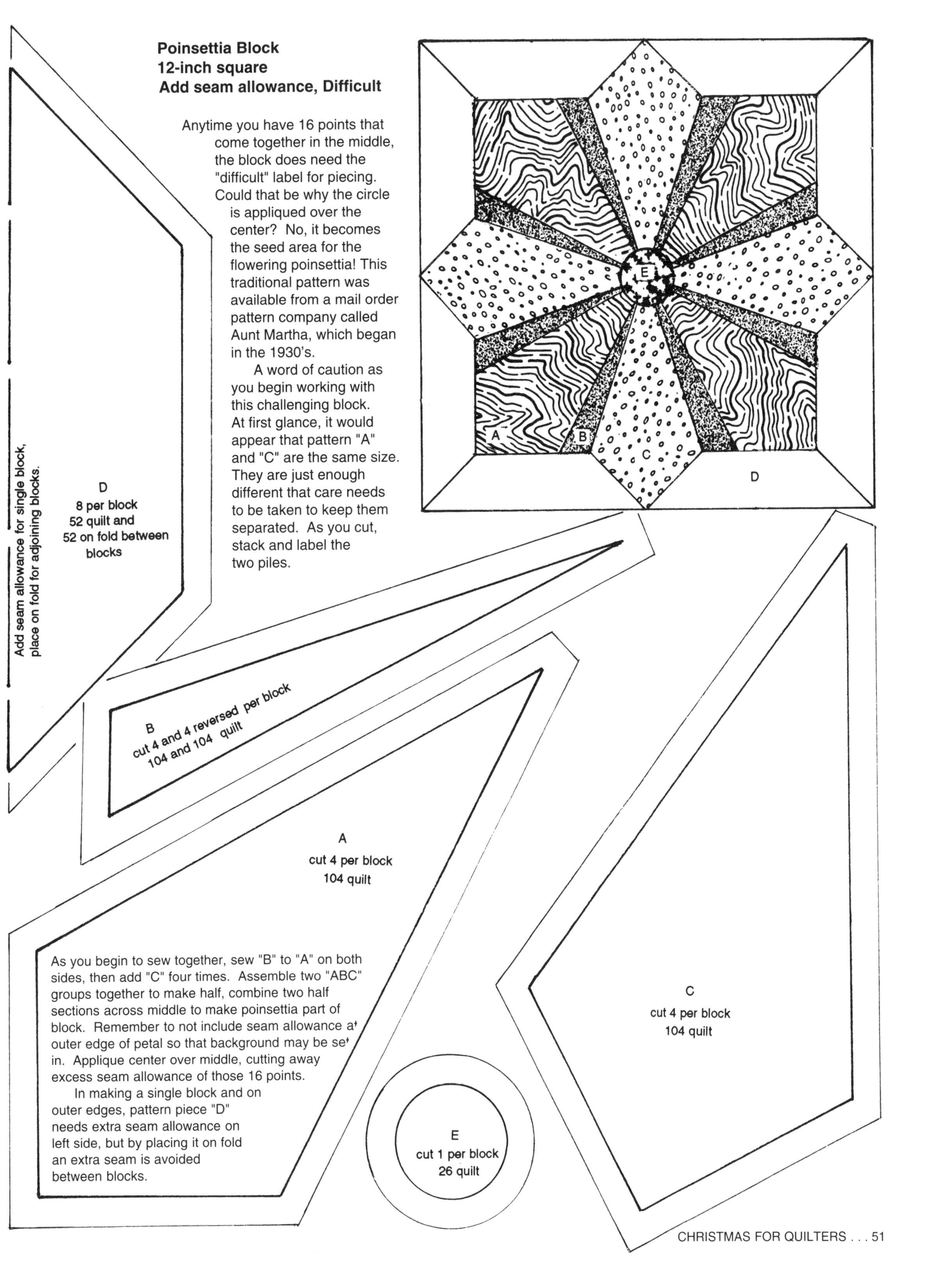

As you begin to sew together, sew "B" to "A" on both sides, then add "C" four times. Assemble two "ABC" groups together to make half, combine two half sections across middle to make poinsettia part of block. Remember to not include seam allowance at outer edge of petal so that background may be set in. Applique center over middle, cutting away excess seam allowance of those 16 points.

In making a single block and on outer edges, pattern piece "D" needs extra seam allowance on left side, but by placing it on fold an extra seam is avoided between blocks.

Basket and Poinsetta Quilt

85 by 106 inches, Medium
Shown in color on back cover

What if you want to make a Christmas quilt, but the room is light blue in color? No problem! But you like red and want your Christmas quilt to have poinsettia as a part of the design. No problem! Red and blue might not be normally compatible, but make interesting contrasts for quiltmaking. Careful choice of pattern, color intensity in the fabrics and a strong border fabric can make that perfect "blue" Christmas quilt. One look at the color photograph tells you that it is a Christmas quilt! I was fortunate to find fabric with a deep blue background. Dark green holly leaves with deep cranberry red in the print helped coordinate the entire quilt.

The blocks are set on point so that the basket sits upright on the bed. The easily pieced alternating block softly fills the other blocks with design yet does not detract from the main basket blocks. The Pinwheel was chosen for its flower like appearance. You may consider other non-traditional alternating blocks.

Three inch sashing divides the blocks. The light/dark/light blue sash is strip pieced into three strips per 3 inch section to add depth to the blocks. Intersections of the sashing are made of 4 triangles alternating dark to medium across the quilt. The dark/medium fabric is the same as used in the basket, however not the same size triangle template. Use "I" triangle size.

To make, piece the 20 pinwheel blocks per block sketch. Piece the 12 basket blocks adding the applique work. The flower was designed with all points coming together so that you could machine applique if you wish.

Continued on Page 53

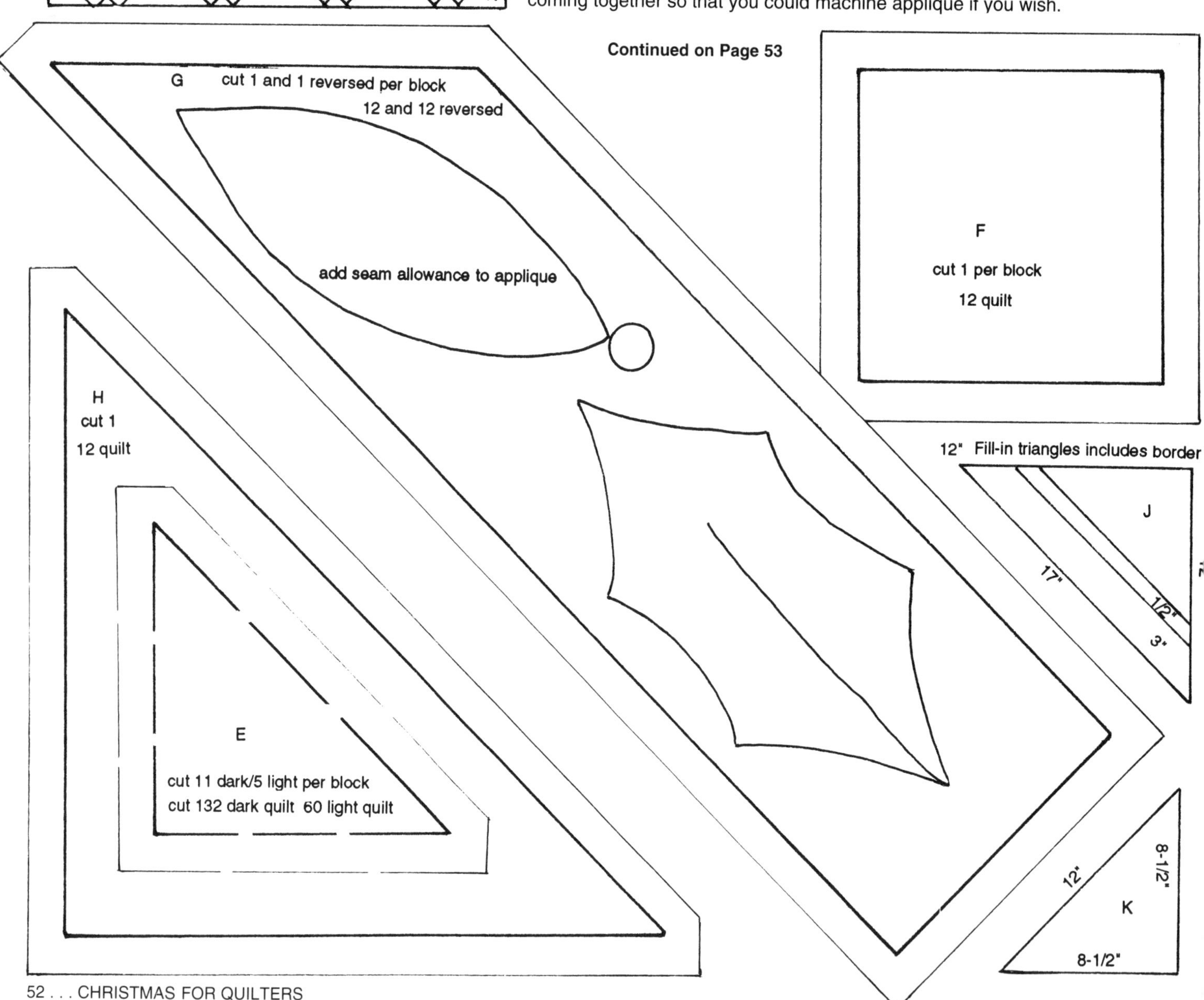

Continued from Page 52

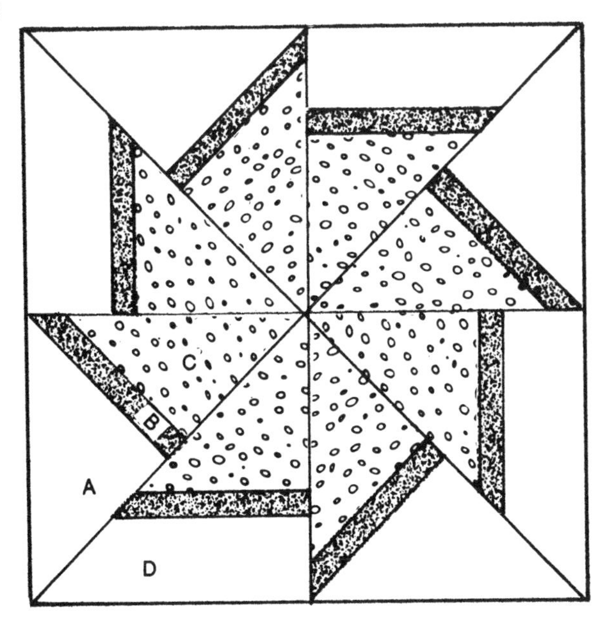

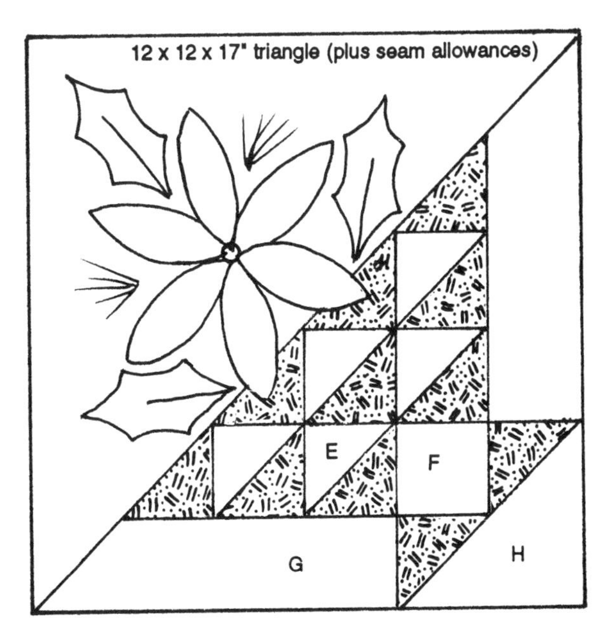

Have seam allowances pressed under firmly in position. Points leave small circle center. Starting in the center, move from one point to the next around the 6 petal red fabric without stopping the thread. Applique a tiny gold center in position and add the leaves.

Make sashing strips. You will need 80 strips, 3 by 12 inches. To make 3 strips, cut across width of fabric 38" by 1-1/2 inches (to measure 1 inch wide after seam allowance) 27 times on all three fabrics. From each 38" set of three, you can cut out 3 strips cutting them 12-1/2 inches which includes the seam allowance. Piece the connecting corners (I). Fourteen outer edge fill-in triangles need to be prepared. Draw out the full triangle size given (J). Divide into the 3 inch border width, 1/2 inch small red highlight and remainder area becomes white background. Cut apart your prepared triangle into the 3 pattern pieces. You will need to add seam allowance to these pieces. Cut 4 corner triangles per measurements in "K" sketch. You are ready to lay out the quilt to start assembling in rows beginning in one corner.

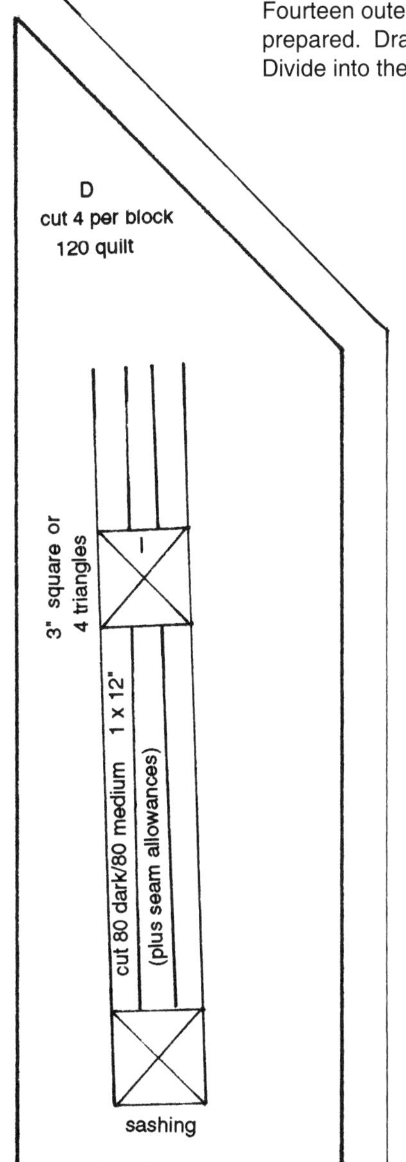

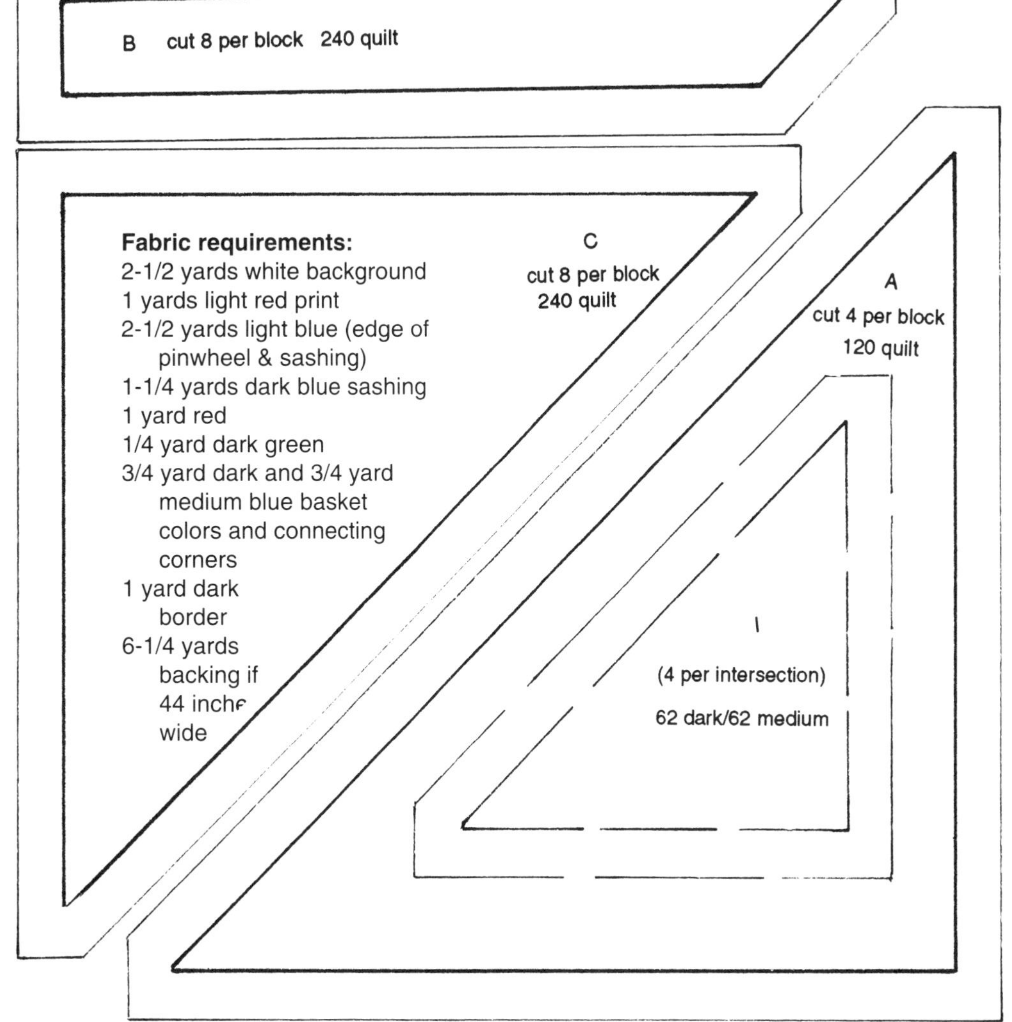

Fabric requirements:

2-1/2 yards white background
1 yards light red print
2-1/2 yards light blue (edge of pinwheel & sashing)
1-1/4 yards dark blue sashing
1 yard red
1/4 yard dark green
3/4 yard dark and 3/4 yard medium blue basket colors and connecting corners
1 yard dark border
6-1/4 yards backing if 44 inche wide

Basic Tree Skirt Instructions:

Right after Christmas is an ideal time to start a new tree skirt since the size could be checked while your tree is still in place. Also, it satisfies the "itchin' to stitch" in a relaxed time after the holiday rush. And there is no immediate deadline! The next five pages include tree skirts with different sizes, difficulty levels, and decorative looks.

It is important to think about color choices ... red/green typical holiday colors versus the color scheme that would look better in the room. Note the blue fan tree skirt that was made to fit the room on color page 39. It emphasizes blue with a touch of green that works better in the room than holiday shade of green.

Christmas tree skirts make excellent gifts, especially wedding gifts. They can be shipped across the country without worry of breakage; and are seldom thought about so are not a duplicate gift. Make as a birthday gift so that they are available for early holiday use.

Other decisions enter in the process besides which pattern to choose. The outer edge finishing! Lace adds a more delicate look. The double/triple lace was used on both of the fan samples. A little heavier looking edge trim is available in a fringe with a visual example on the star design tree skirt on page 39. Or, you may choose to simply bind off the tree skirt as was done on the Rosalia Flower Garden/Jack's Chain pieced skirt.

A red fabric ruffle was added to the triangle tree skirt as an option for finishing off the outer edge. A 3 inch finished ruffle is a good width. Cut fabric 6-1/2 inches wide, fold in half, press and gather raw edges. Cut 6-1/2 inches across width of fabric 7 times to make about 8 yards of 3 inch finished ruffling. It takes 1-3/8 yards of ruffle fabric to go around a tree skirt. Divide into sections to evenly place gathers around tree skirt.

The 8 diamonds of the star tree skirt require a 12 inch block to fill the openings. This means that any and all of the 12 inch blocks in the book could be used. Design your own tree skirt!

To make tree skirt top, use a very light weight batting and backing which makes for easier storage. Cut backing and batting a little larger size than the tree skirt. It is easier to mark the slit before layering together. If lace is used that fits into the seam, stitch in position on top. With batting backed up to top, front and back right sides together, stitch around complete outer edge. Turn tree skirt to outside. Lightly press outer edge.

It is at this point that quilting should be done. You may choose to machine quilt, but extra care needs to be taken to avoid shifting the three layers. It is easier to quilt if left in a complete circle. Try to quilt as many lines toward the center opening hole as possible so any shifting can be corrected before binding off. When quilting is done, cut a 4-1/2 to 6 inch diameter circle in center and slit to outer edge. Bind off center circle and slit with a bias binding of 2 yards long by 2 inches wide. On the diamond star tree skirt, the slit is down the middle of one diamond, which does not disturb the block fill-in design. Look at the design to carefully choose where the slit should go.

Fold binding in half lengthwise, press and stitch on front, turn to back to hand stitch in position. Now is the time to add lace or fringe that goes on the outer edge, which does not need to be caught in the seam.

Triangle Tree Skirt
40 inch plus ruffle
Add seam allowance, Easy
Shown in color on page 39

Eight wedge shapes filled with rows of triangles are all it takes to make a tree skirt. Choose bright holiday fabrics and colors, or choose a color grouping that coordinates with the colors of the room where the tree is located.

Make rows of triangles to form wedge, sew wedge sections together to form tree skirt. Leave one open. Once all together, cut a 4-1/2 inch diameter circle in the center. Refer to the general assembly instructions above. A 3 inch wide ruffle finishes the edge of the triangle skirt shown in color top left of page 39 .

Fabric requirements:
- 3/8 yard of 8 fabrics for triangles
- 1-3/4 yards to make ruffle & binding off
- 1-3/4 yards backing fabric

To make a single wedge,
measure out 20" from this beginning angle

cut 25 per wedge
100 every other wedge
200 all eight wedges

45 degree diamond makes octagon shape.

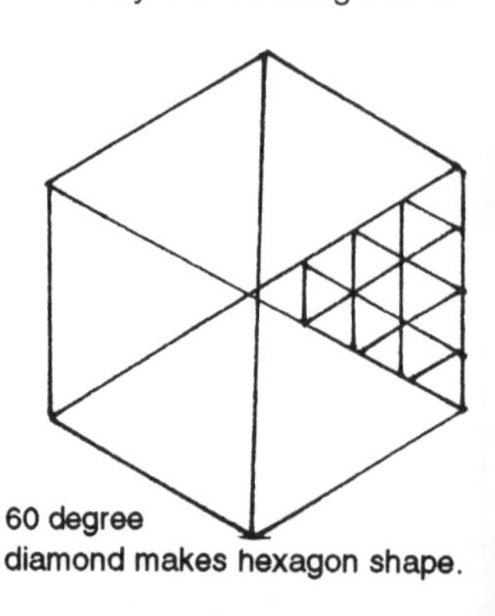

60 degree
diamond makes hexagon shape.

Rosalia Flower Garden Jack's Chain Tree Skirt

55 inches at widest part
Add seam allowance, Medium
Shown in color on page 39

The Rosalia Flower Garden pattern was featured in the1939 Kansas City Star newspaper. Another source refers to the very same design as Jack's Chain pattern. The pattern consists of three shapes: a larger center hexagon, triangles that encircle the hexagon and squares of nine patch blocks. It is this larger center hexagon shape that gave me the idea of using it for a tree skirt. The center hexagon is eliminated and bound off, continuing down around pattern shape as shown in sketch to form the opening slit. If a 12 inch opening is too large, make a smaller circle in middle of hexagon.

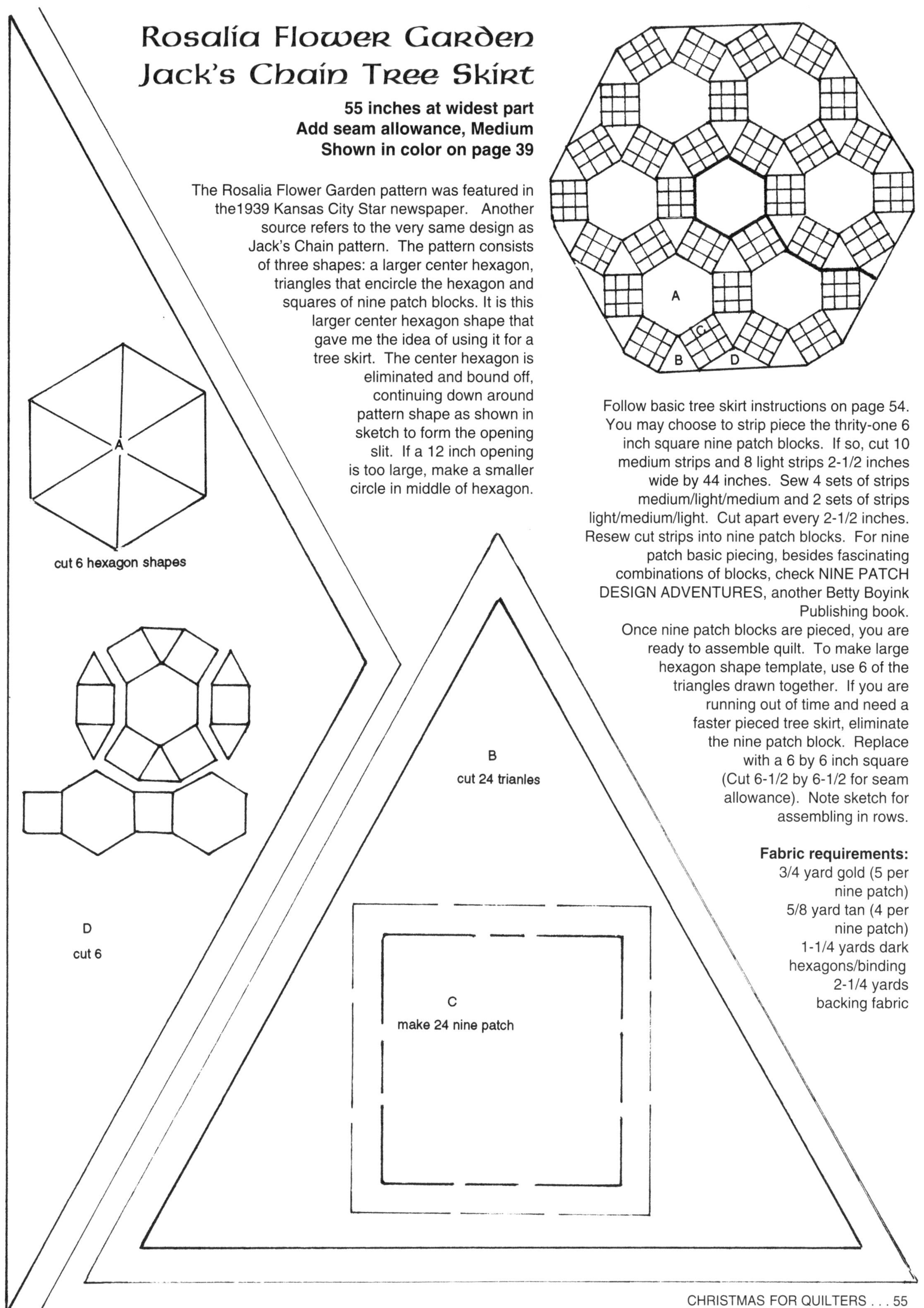

Follow basic tree skirt instructions on page 54. You may choose to strip piece the thrity-one 6 inch square nine patch blocks. If so, cut 10 medium strips and 8 light strips 2-1/2 inches wide by 44 inches. Sew 4 sets of strips medium/light/medium and 2 sets of strips light/medium/light. Cut apart every 2-1/2 inches. Resew cut strips into nine patch blocks. For nine patch basic piecing, besides fascinating combinations of blocks, check NINE PATCH DESIGN ADVENTURES, another Betty Boyink Publishing book.

Once nine patch blocks are pieced, you are ready to assemble quilt. To make large hexagon shape template, use 6 of the triangles drawn together. If you are running out of time and need a faster pieced tree skirt, eliminate the nine patch block. Replace with a 6 by 6 inch square (Cut 6-1/2 by 6-1/2 for seam allowance). Note sketch for assembling in rows.

Fabric requirements:
3/4 yard gold (5 per nine patch)
5/8 yard tan (4 per nine patch)
1-1/4 yards dark hexagons/binding
2-1/4 yards backing fabric

Star Tree Skirt & Table Cover

41 and 58 inches circumference
Add seam allowance
Shown in color on pages 38-39

The 8 point diamond star makes a great tree skirt. In its simplest form, it can be the 8 diamonds filled in with 8 triangles (view "c"). This makes a smaller and easier to make tree skirt or table top. Or, a square can fill in around the diamonds for a tree skirt as the one shown in color on page 39 (view "b"). Measurements are given for you to draw out. Add seam allowance to each pattern as you make template.

Eight different coordinated holiday print fabrics were used for this version. The 8 diamonds are framed with 8 dark green triangles. The outer half of the square or triangle is divided, which gives a light triangle framed with two darker colors. See sketch of block. View "a" has triangles that fill in around the squares to make an octagon shape.

To make the star template, use the measurements and angles given for full size paper template. Add seam allowance to your template. Cut out 8 star points sewing them together leaving outer edge free so that the block may be set into corners. To make fill in triangle, use actual size measurements given for template, adding seam allowance. Follow basic tree skirt instructions on page 54.

Fabric requirements:

3/8 yard 8 holiday prints, 5/8 yard if 4 prints are used
3/4 yard dark green
1-1/4 yards backing small size, 2 yards larger size
Outer edge trims require 5-1/2 yards if added after squares and elongated trianlges (view "a"), 5-3/4 yards if added after squares that fill in around diamonds (view "b"), or 4-1/4 yards lace if added after triangles (view "c"),

12"
12"
9 1/8"
12"
12"

A 58 inch diameter

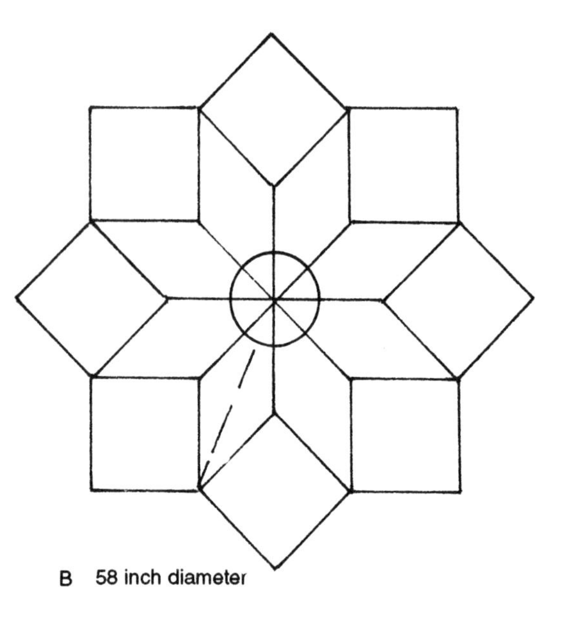

B 58 inch diameter

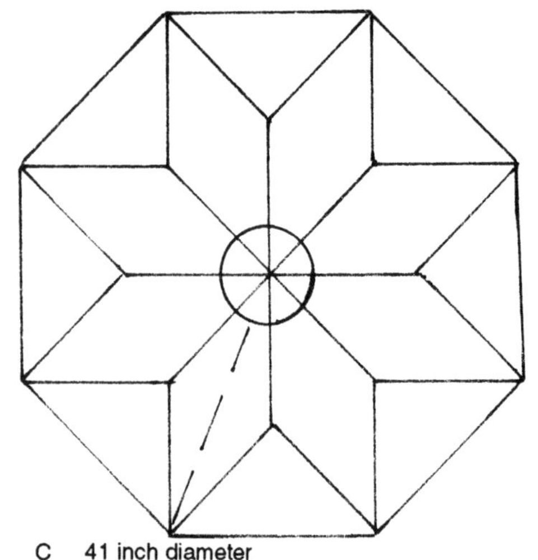

C 41 inch diameter

measure out 12" from this starting angle

12 inch fill in block.

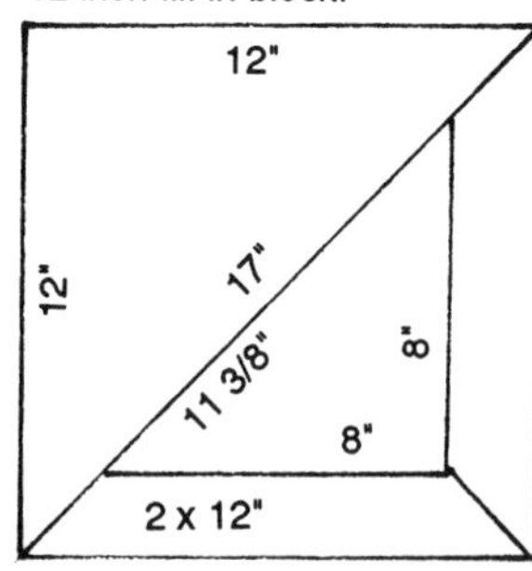

Fan Tree Skirt

48 inch Diameter (plus lace), 12 inch fan
Add seam allowance, Easy
Shown in color on page 39

A

C

B

place on fold

A fan combined with the popular 8 point star makes for an easy and fairly fast pieced tree skirt. The curved edge of the fan adds to the tree skirt's beauty in the rounded outer edge. Our fan has a 3 inch center and 6 inch petals making it a 9 inch fan with the outer 3 inches creating a border effect. Note on color page, that two tree skirts use the fan/star pattern. On botton right tree skirt on page 39, the border is a solid fabric with appliqued holly leaves and button berries. The top right photo shows us that the outer border can be the same fabric as star. The other difference is in the top right skirt, the fan petals are carefully cut from a stripe fabric giving a curved flow as the petals move around.

To make tree skirt, cut 6 petals per fan, having a total of 48 petals. If you use 6 different fabrics and position the petals in different places on each fan, it makes a more interesting set. Stitch petals together, adding fan base and outer border. If applique is added, now is the time while block is still small. Follow basic tree skirt instructions on page 54.

C

cut 6 per fan
48 total

A

cut 8

B

cut 8

Fabric requirements:
1 yard diamond star points
1/4 yard 6 fabrics fan petals
1/2 yard outer border (if same as star point fabric, get 1/4 yard)
1-3/4 yards backing
5-1/2 yards lace, fringe, ruffle

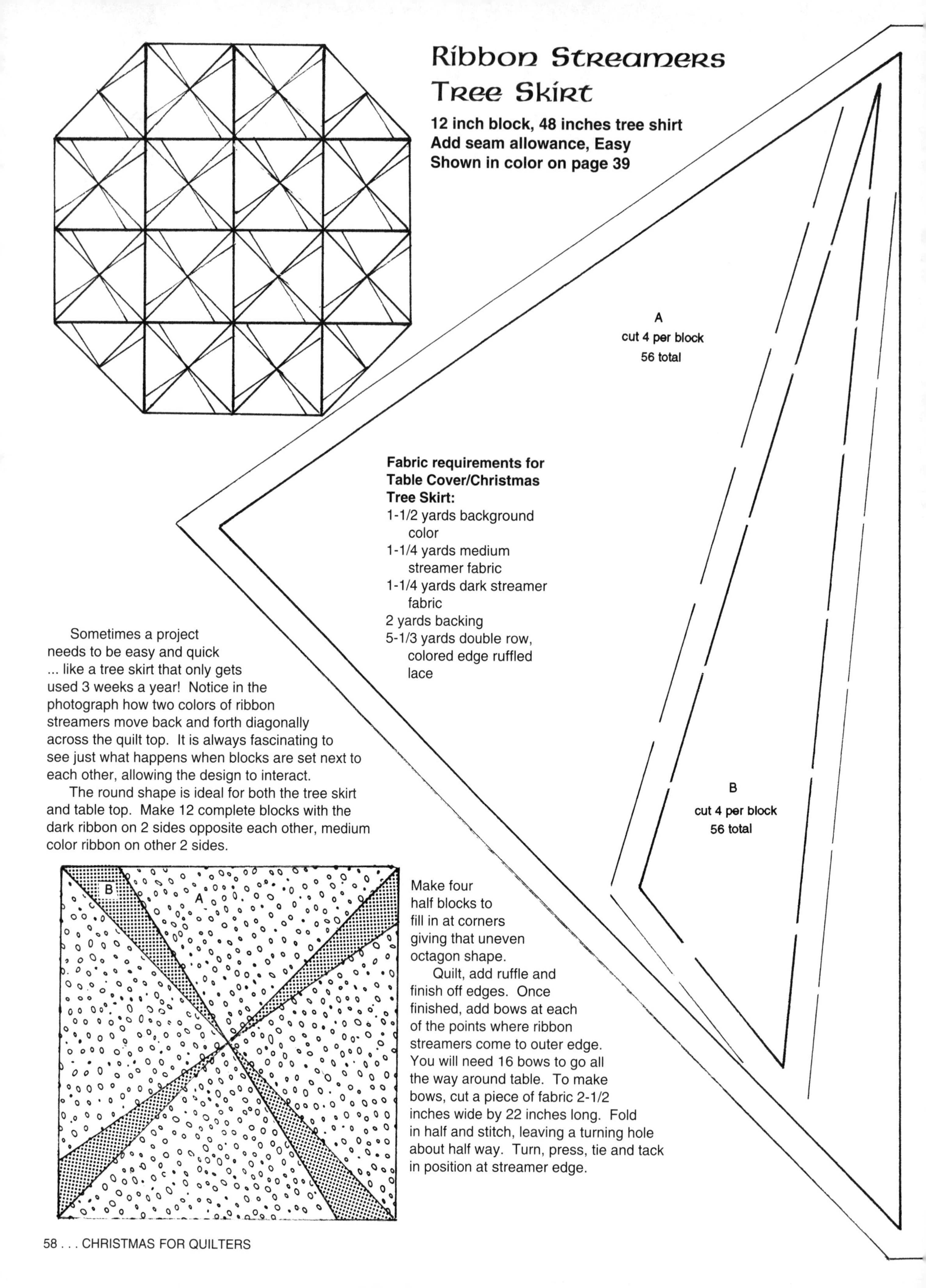

Ribbon Streamers Tree Skirt

12 inch block, 48 inches tree shirt
Add seam allowance, Easy
Shown in color on page 39

Fabric requirements for Table Cover/Christmas Tree Skirt:

1-1/2 yards background color
1-1/4 yards medium streamer fabric
1-1/4 yards dark streamer fabric
2 yards backing
5-1/3 yards double row, colored edge ruffled lace

Sometimes a project needs to be easy and quick ... like a tree skirt that only gets used 3 weeks a year! Notice in the photograph how two colors of ribbon streamers move back and forth diagonally across the quilt top. It is always fascinating to see just what happens when blocks are set next to each other, allowing the design to interact.

The round shape is ideal for both the tree skirt and table top. Make 12 complete blocks with the dark ribbon on 2 sides opposite each other, medium color ribbon on other 2 sides.

Make four half blocks to fill in at corners giving that uneven octagon shape.

Quilt, add ruffle and finish off edges. Once finished, add bows at each of the points where ribbon streamers come to outer edge. You will need 16 bows to go all the way around table. To make bows, cut a piece of fabric 2-1/2 inches wide by 22 inches long. Fold in half and stitch, leaving a turning hole about half way. Turn, press, tie and tack in position at streamer edge.

ift Box Ornament
dd seam allowance, Easy

Gift Box Ornament 4 inch size pattern is on page 60 . A row of boxes makes an xcellent border for holiday quilts as illustrated on the Twelve Days of Christmas iece seen in color on page 36. It is best to use three different values of the same olor to give the best depth perception for a true box look. As you sew the three 60 egree diamonds together, add a piece of ribbon as illustrated. Once box is made, se the whole sketch (adding seam allowance) for batting and backing pattern.

ove Ornament
dd seam allowance, Easy
hown in color on page 39

All white doves on a tree can make a real statement of simplicity. The dove has ong been used during the holidays with several symbolisms possible. The dove as become a symbol of peace which is often the hope of the holidays. New nternational Version, Matthew 3, verse 16, "As soon as Jesus was baptized, he vent up out of the water. At that moment heaven was opened, and he saw the pirit of God descending like a dove and lighting on him. And a voice from heaven aid, 'This is my Son, whom I love; with him I am well pleased.'"

To make an ornament, cut two layers of the whole dove shape adding seam llowance and a firm batting. With right sides together, place batting on bottom to o under sewing machine feed dogs, stitch in 1/4 inch seam allowance leaving urning opening. Reinforce with back stitch at beginning and ending of turning hole. lake two dove wings in the same manner adding batting as you stitch together. urn all three pieces. Hand stitch openings closed. You may either machine or and quilt feather dividing lines both on wings and tail for added definition. Pictured ample uses a silver metalic thread for a touch of sparkle as the lights of the tree hit hat area. Position wings at angles illustrated, one on each side of dove lip-stitching in place. A silver or green thread attached at top back position makes good hanger. Should you want a more delicate, smaller size dove, use the pattern om the Twelve Days of Christmas. Remember that the smaller size will require reater care and be more difficult to turn.

8 - Maids a-milking

leave open between slash marks for turning

leave open between slash marks for turning

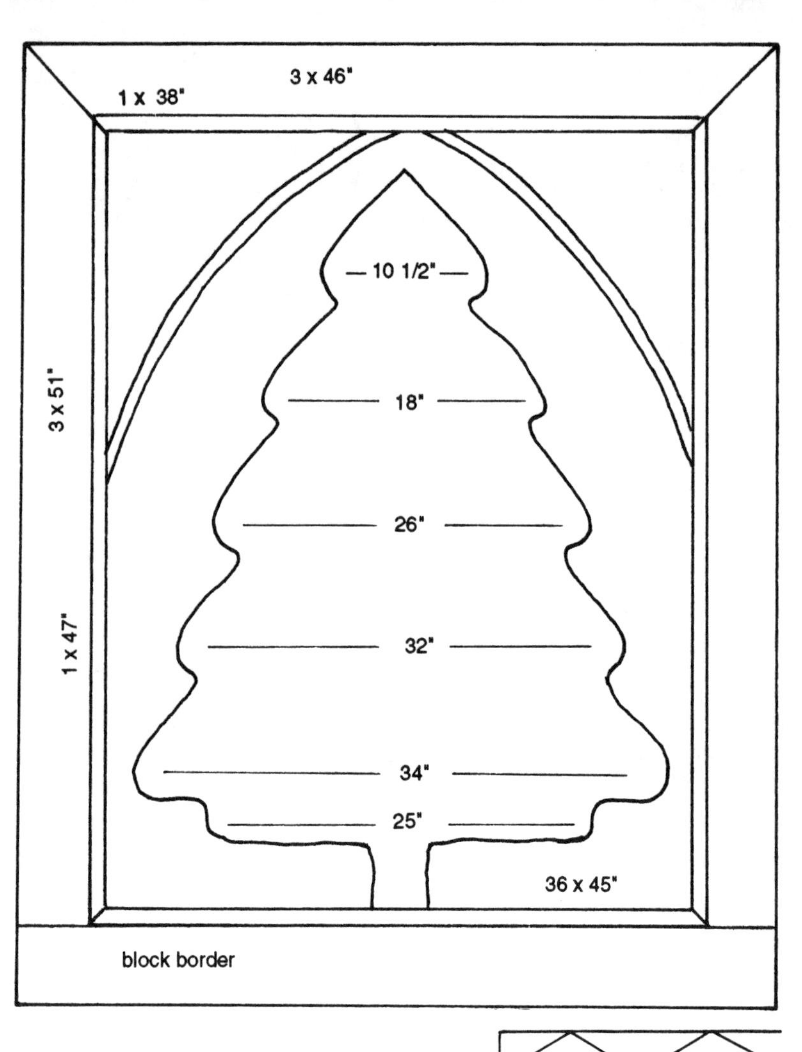

Twelve Days of Christmas

46 by 55 inches
Add seam allowance, Difficult
Shown in color on page 36
Fabric Requirements on page 64

What person, from a child right on through the adult years, doesn't remember fondly singing the Twelve Days of Christmas rhyme? Maybe it is the partridge in the pear tree one envisions that brings the smile or the five golden rings with its slower tempo that is the delight. Or the repetitiveness that allows even very young children to remember the verses. Perhaps it is even trying to remember which subject fits with each number. Whatever the reason, this traditional English folk song has been enjoyed by many and illustrated by artists from all mediums.

If we think of decorating our tree with the twelve days of Christmas theme, we need to make ornaments of the scenes. This illustrated version of the folk song was done with the applique stitcher in mind... most of the time. There are some areas that have small pieces to applique, in order to portray the scene that tells the story. You may choose to embroider the scenes.

The tree shape with instructions is given on page 62. The whole circle ornament shape is given on page 61. Cut your ornament background fabric 8 inches square. It is easier to applique or embroider on the square. This gives room for a small embroidery hoop for those fine details.

You will notice that some of the background pieces seem to have a shape across the full width. The addition of another color moving across the background adds the circling effect to the tall, slim designs of the higher "number of days" characters.

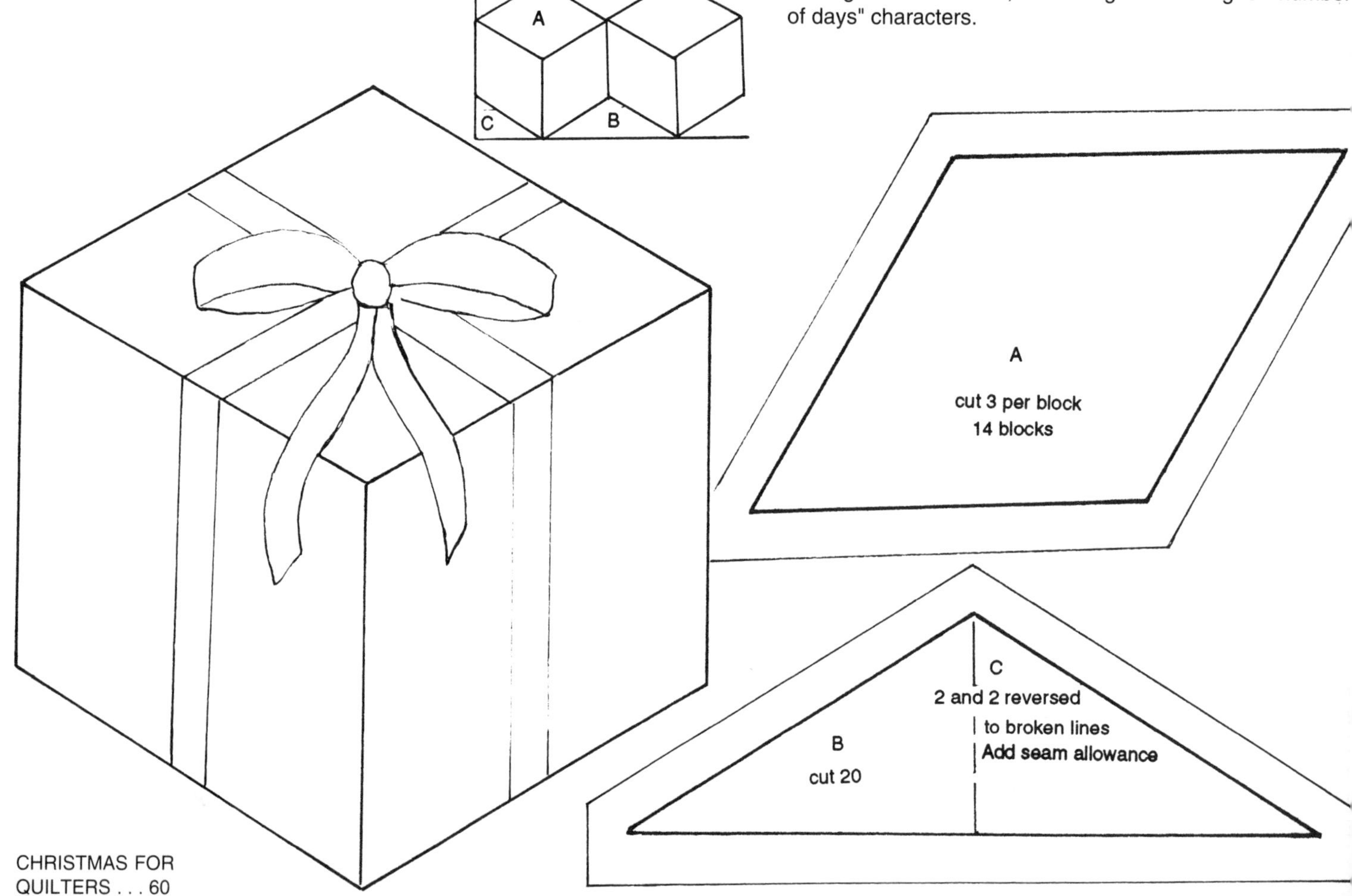

Use the designs on the following pages to make your pattern pieces. Once a scene f pattern pieces and applique pieces are prepared, put them in an envelope to keep eparated until stitched in place. Choose the applique method you prefer.

For our sample, reverse applique method of putting the ornament on the tree was sed. The tree is appliqued on background first, then carefully cut away background om behind the tree shape to get rid of the extra layer of bulk. On the vrong side of the tree, mark the twelve circles using the color hotograph as a guide for placement. Cut the circle 1/4 inch seam llowance smaller than the actual circle. It is easier if a window emplate is drawn actual size. Note broken lines on circle. Cut one t a time, stitching scene in place before cutting out next circle. Once cene is stitched in place underneath tree circle, excess from the riginal 8 inch square can be cut away.

Note the touch of red piping that highlights each ornament circle. This is optional, ut adds a more definitive line around the ornaments. To make, piping has to be on the ias since it curves. Cut 12 pieces of bias 1/2 inch wide by 22 inches long. Machine aste in position around the circle so that once circle is attached to ornament ackground bias is in position.

Once all ornaments are in position, the red curve 1 inch inner border is appliqued in osition. Add the outer borders using the measurements from the sketch. The gift box rnament pattern is on page 60.

Applique the pears in the opening. You may choose to eliminate the curve area that helps fill in near the top of he tapered tree.

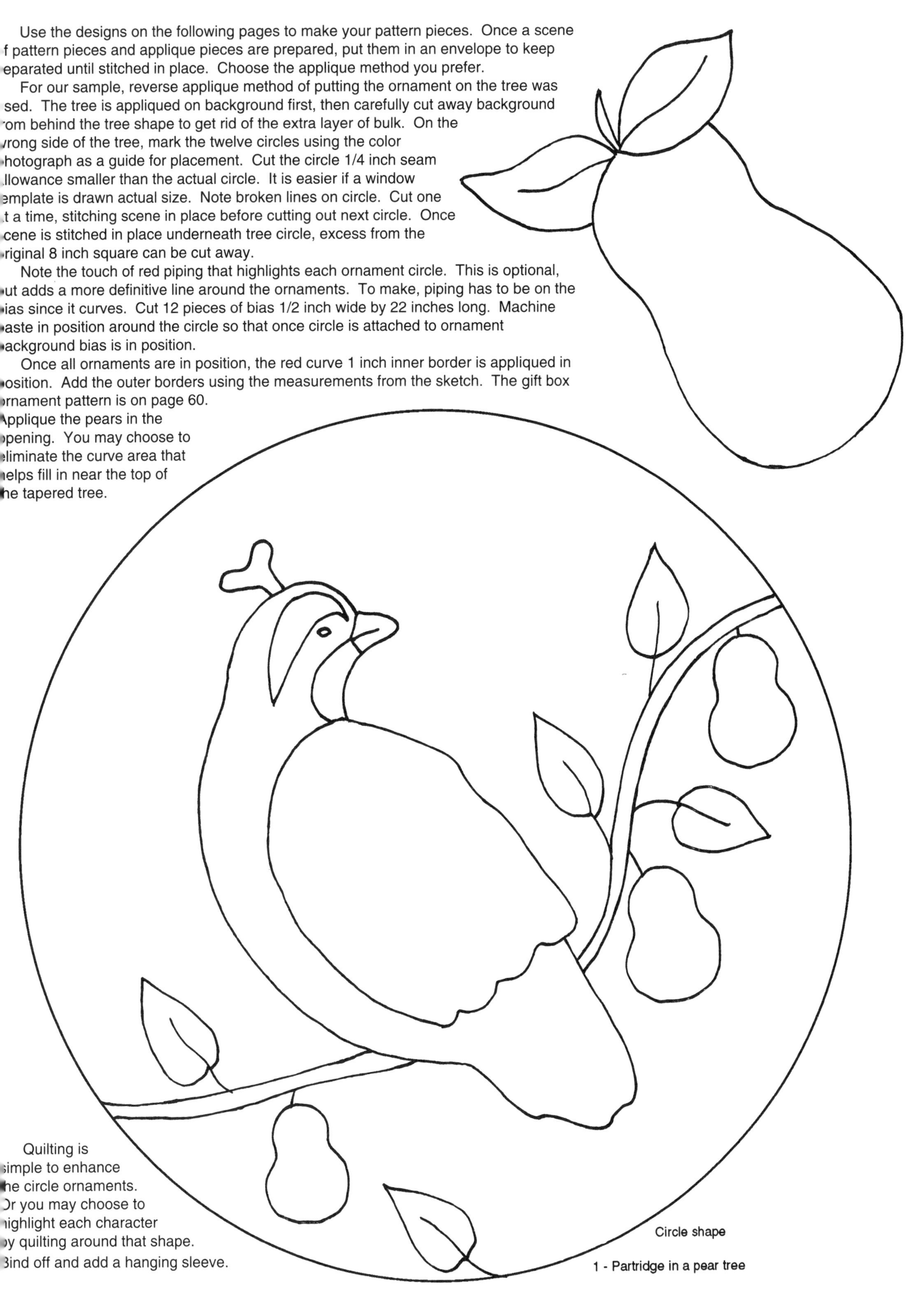

Circle shape

1 - Partridge in a pear tree

Quilting is simple to enhance he circle ornaments. Or you may choose to highlight each character by quilting around that shape. Bind off and add a hanging sleeve.

On the twelth day of Christmas
My true love sent to me
Twelve drummers drumming,
Eleven pipers piping,
Ten lords a-leaping,
Nine ladies dancing,
Eight maids a-milking,
Seven swans a-swimming,
Six geese a-laying,
Five golden rings,
Four calling birds,
Three French hens,
Two turtle doves,
And a partridge in a pear tree.

Making Tree Shape
Height 44 inches
Width at bottom branches 34 inches

As the tree enlarges after the tree top section, a method has been devised for making a perfectly shaped tree with the boughs the same distance apart. Note the pointed top is on the fold. Using a piece of paper 36 x45 inches, make a mark down the middle. Center the pattern 1 inch from upper edge of paper using tree top shape in book. For each succeeding bough, use the same shape as the top pattern. Position in place the outer edge of the bough, extending out from center line using measurements given on page 60. Continue on down for five boughs with each section about 8 inches down. Note the smaller portion before the tree trunk is about 3 inches. Tree trunk is 3-1/2 by 3-1/2 inches and can be included with tree shape or could be a separate piece of fabric.

Note how the top curve in quilt sketch provides a finished look (also seen in color photo). Draw this on paper for an exact pattern. This way it can be pieced rather than appliqued.

11 - Pipers piping
9-Ladies dancing
2 - Turtle doves
3 - French hens

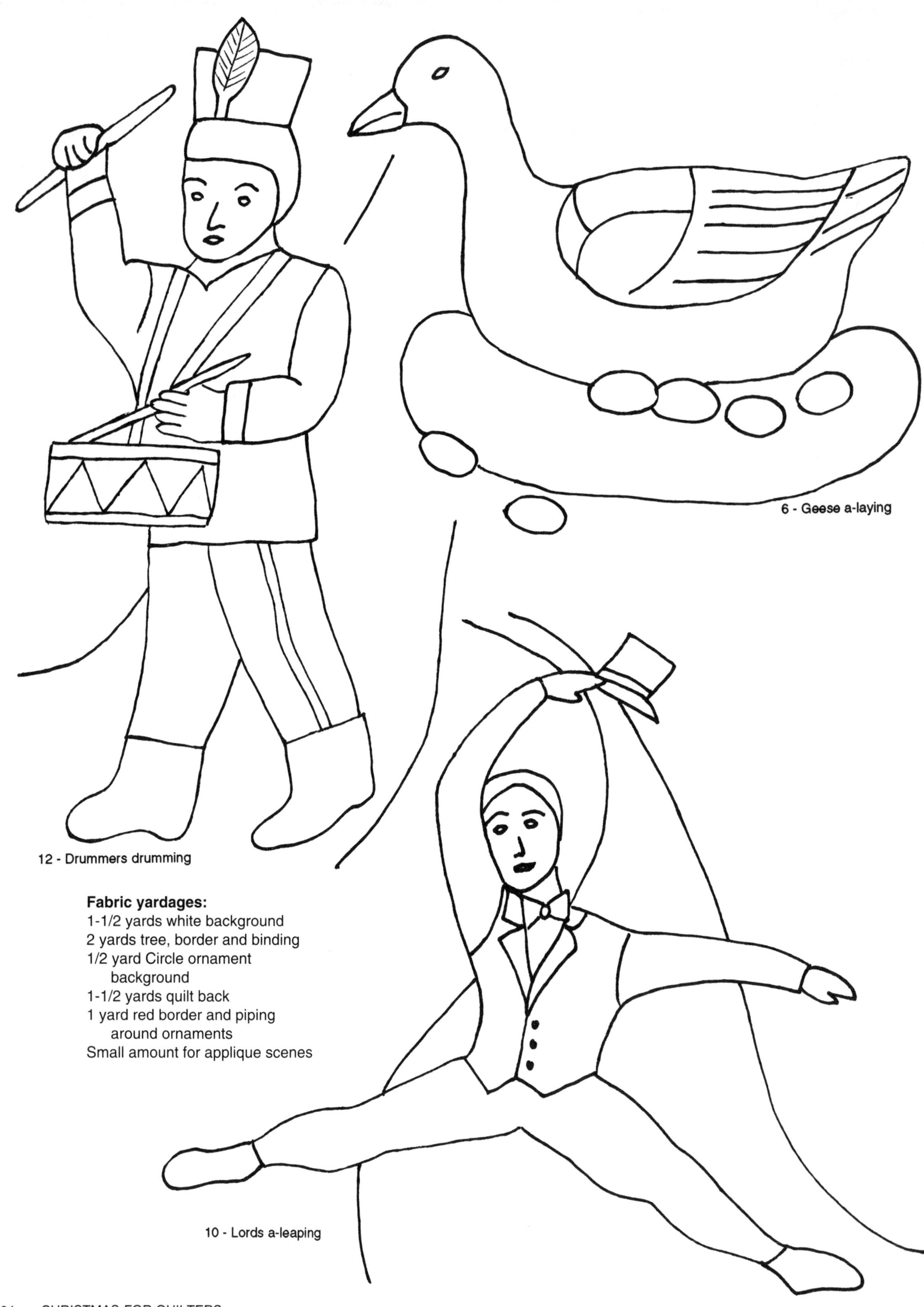

6 - Geese a-laying

12 - Drummers drumming

10 - Lords a-leaping

Fabric yardages:
1-1/2 yards white background
2 yards tree, border and binding
1/2 yard Circle ornament background
1-1/2 yards quilt back
1 yard red border and piping around ornaments
Small amount for applique scenes

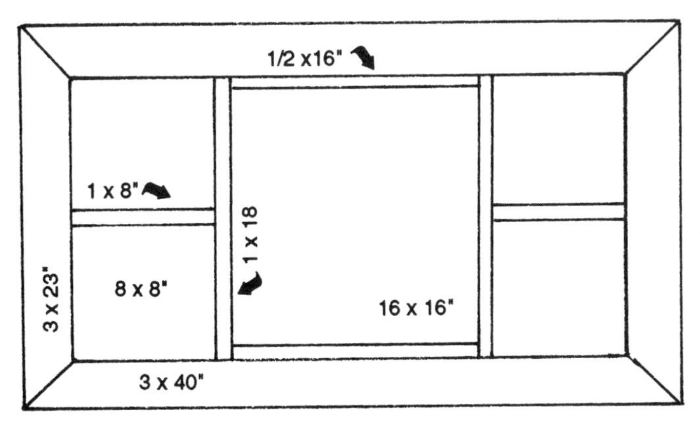

Holiday Sampler

23 x 40 inches
Add seam allowance
Shown in color on page 38

Five blocks make a delightful holiday sampler! Two are Christmas Star blocks. Two have poinsettia designs, one of which is combined with a basket in an arrangement. The fifth one is a tree block. The large diamond design is a 16 inch block with remaining 4 blocks using the 8 inch size. Unlike many wall quilts that hang lengthways, the basket and tree patterns make this Holiday Sampler hang horizontal on the wall.

The basket block is on pages 52-53, tree block is on pages 24-25, large poinsettia is on page 49, and one Christmas star is on this page with the second star on page 67. The measurements in the quilt sketch guide above help divide blocks with sashing strips and add the final framing border. A holly leaf was used to fill in for border quilting detail.

Fabric Requirements:
1-1/4 yards dark green
1 yard white background
1/2 yard medium green
3/4 yard quilt back
Small amount of two each of red and green for blocks

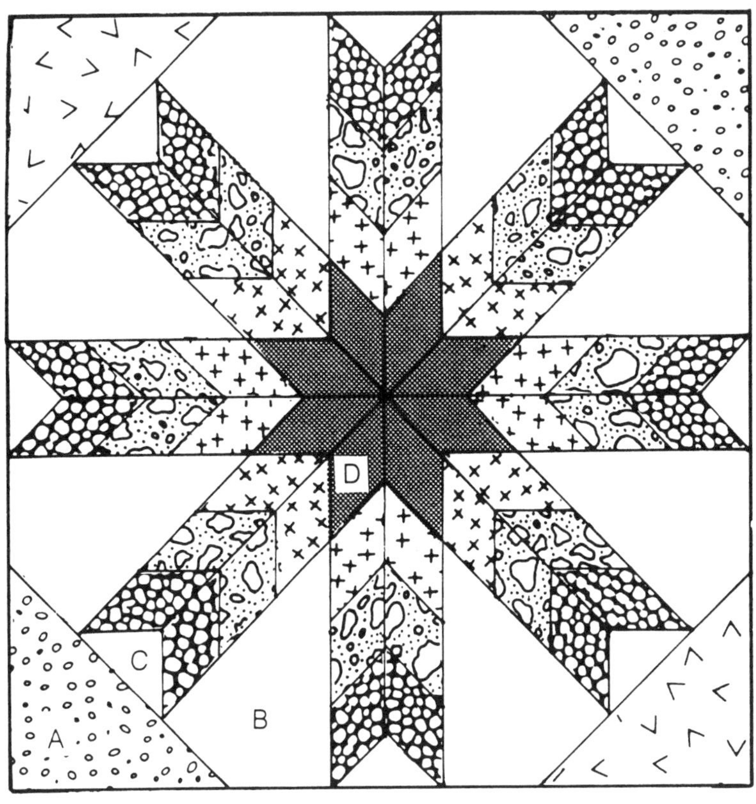

Christmas Star

12 and 16 inch size
Add seam allowance, Difficult

There are two traditional quilt blocks named Christmas Star. Based on the 45 degree diamond shape, this version is a 1931 Kansas City Star Newspaper design. The more difficult one! A guide below shows how the block may be assembled. The other Christmas Star is on page 67. The Holiday Sampler quilt uses the larger 16 inch size, but we've included a 12 inch size for use where that size is required. Due to space and two different sizes, we have not included seam allowance.

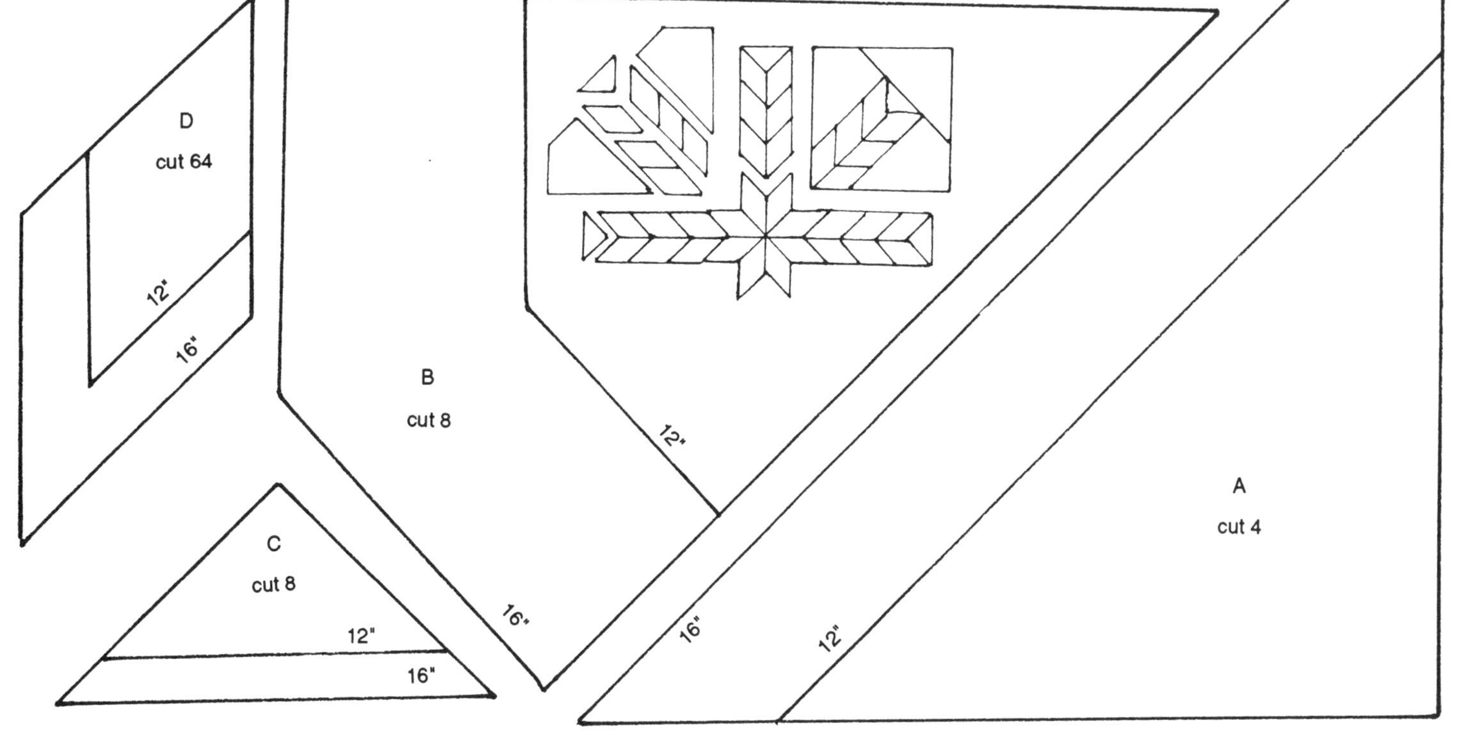

Christmas Star Quilt Bear

Fabric Requirements:
1-1/2 yards coral
1-3/4 yards blue
1 yard brown
1-3/4 yards background
Small amount of bear
and ball colors for
applique

Christmas Star

, 8 and 12 inch size block
8 x 56 inch quilt
Add seam allowance, Medium
Shown in color on inside front cover

Stars shine at Christmas time! Could that be the reason uilters of yesterday named this block design "Christmas Star"? As one of two very different Christmas Star blocks other star block is on page 65), this pattern was featured in 1950 issue of Workbasket.

The pattern section below includes both the 8 and 12 nch size patterns. The 8 inch size was used in Holiday Sampler on page 65 and the 12 inch size was required for ne crib size quilt.

Remember in the introduction, we suggested that Christmas quilts did not always have to be the red/green combination. Blue, brown and a bright coral color were used with this 12 inch block quilt. It seemed the perfect ome for a brown bear to sit while playing with his ball. These were appliqued on the quilt top after the blocks were set together. Milly Splitstone of Fremont, Michigan had acquired the blocks via the group quilt route. They sat a ew years until I put them together and then began to have un adding the bear for that special touch of interest. The addition of 2 borders frame and finish the quilt top. Now it was back to Milly for quilting!

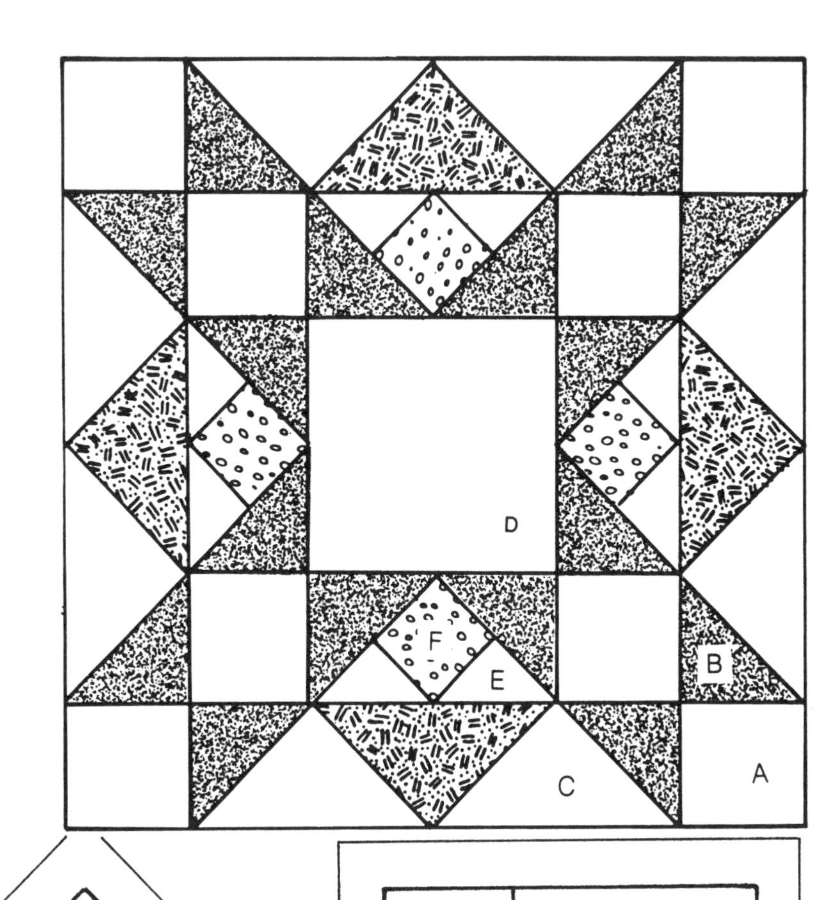

E
cut 8 per block
8"
48 quilt
12"

A
cut 4 per block
48 quilt
8"
12"

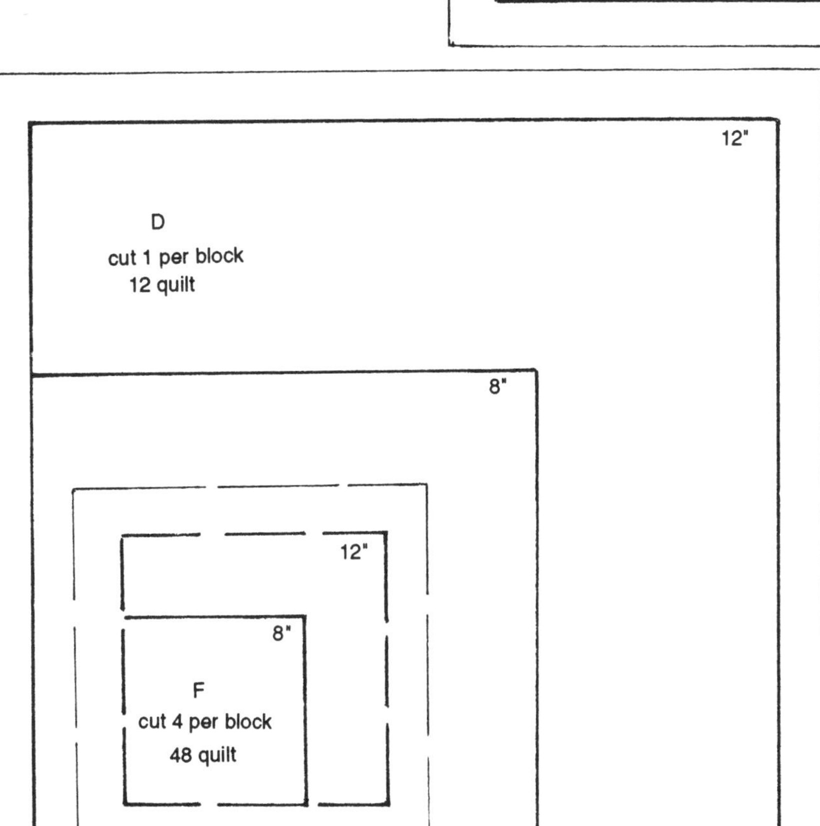

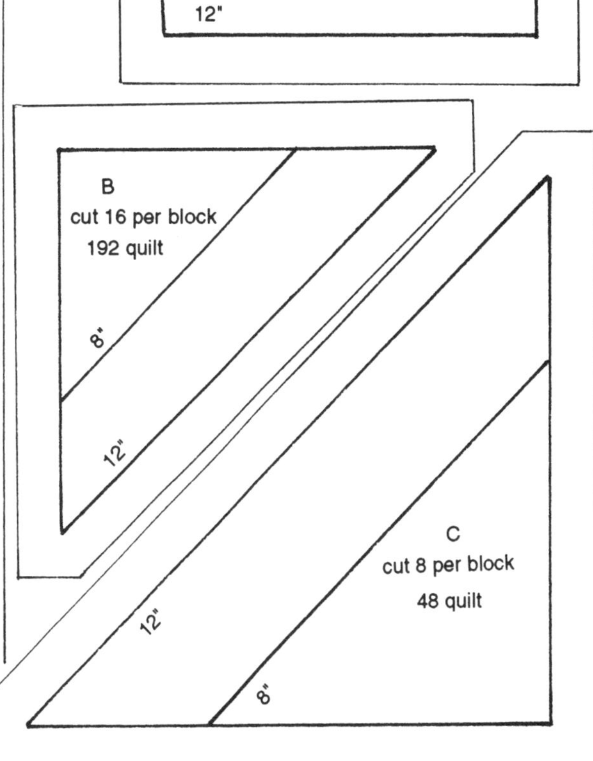

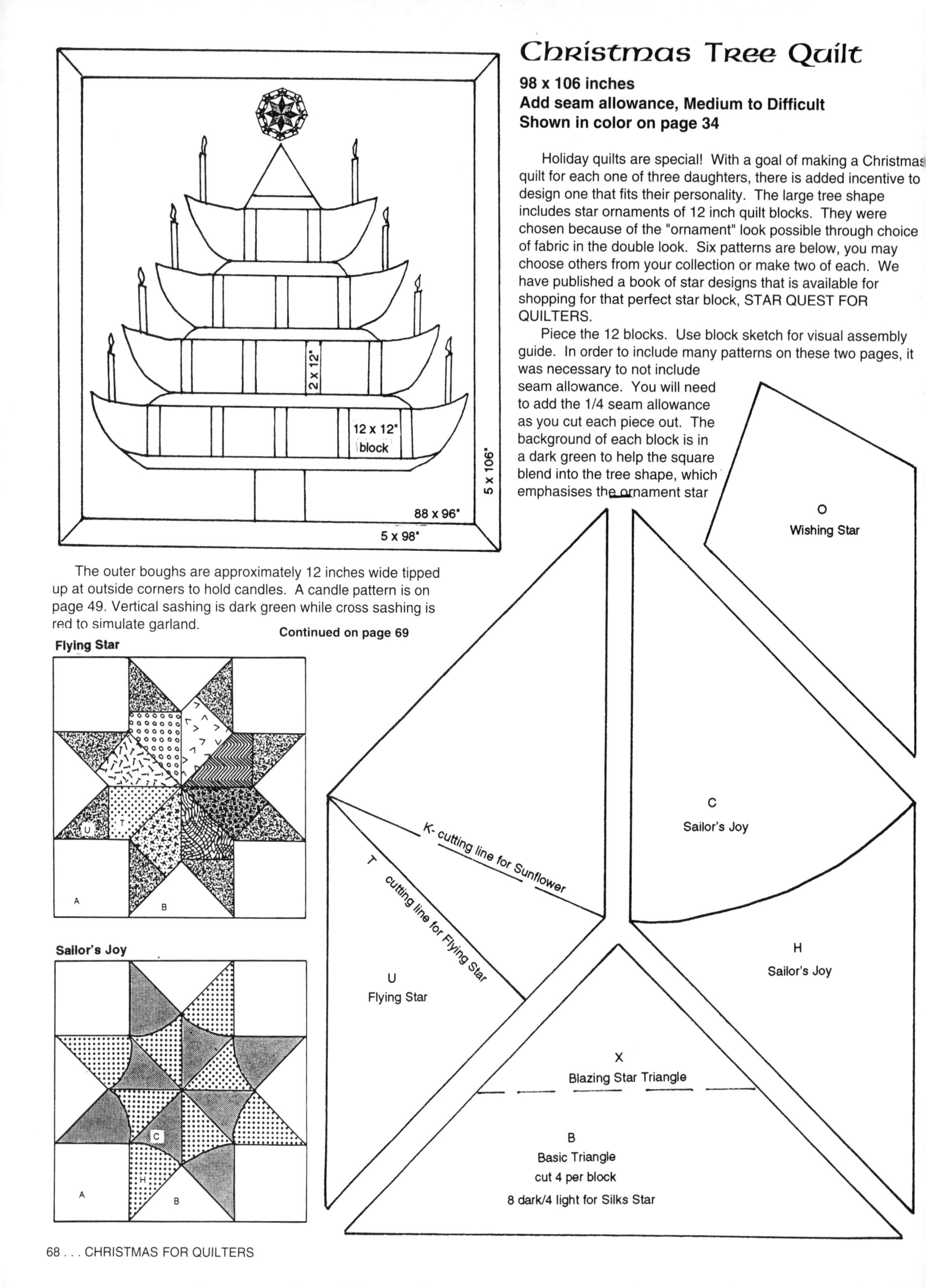

Christmas Tree Quilt

98 x 106 inches
Add seam allowance, Medium to Difficult
Shown in color on page 34

Holiday quilts are special! With a goal of making a Christmas quilt for each one of three daughters, there is added incentive to design one that fits their personality. The large tree shape includes star ornaments of 12 inch quilt blocks. They were chosen because of the "ornament" look possible through choice of fabric in the double look. Six patterns are below, you may choose others from your collection or make two of each. We have published a book of star designs that is available for shopping for that perfect star block, STAR QUEST FOR QUILTERS.

Piece the 12 blocks. Use block sketch for visual assembly guide. In order to include many patterns on these two pages, it was necessary to not include seam allowance. You will need to add the 1/4 seam allowance as you cut each piece out. The background of each block is in a dark green to help the square blend into the tree shape, which emphasises the ornament star

The outer boughs are approximately 12 inches wide tipped up at outside corners to hold candles. A candle pattern is on page 49. Vertical sashing is dark green while cross sashing is red to simulate garland.

Continued on page 69

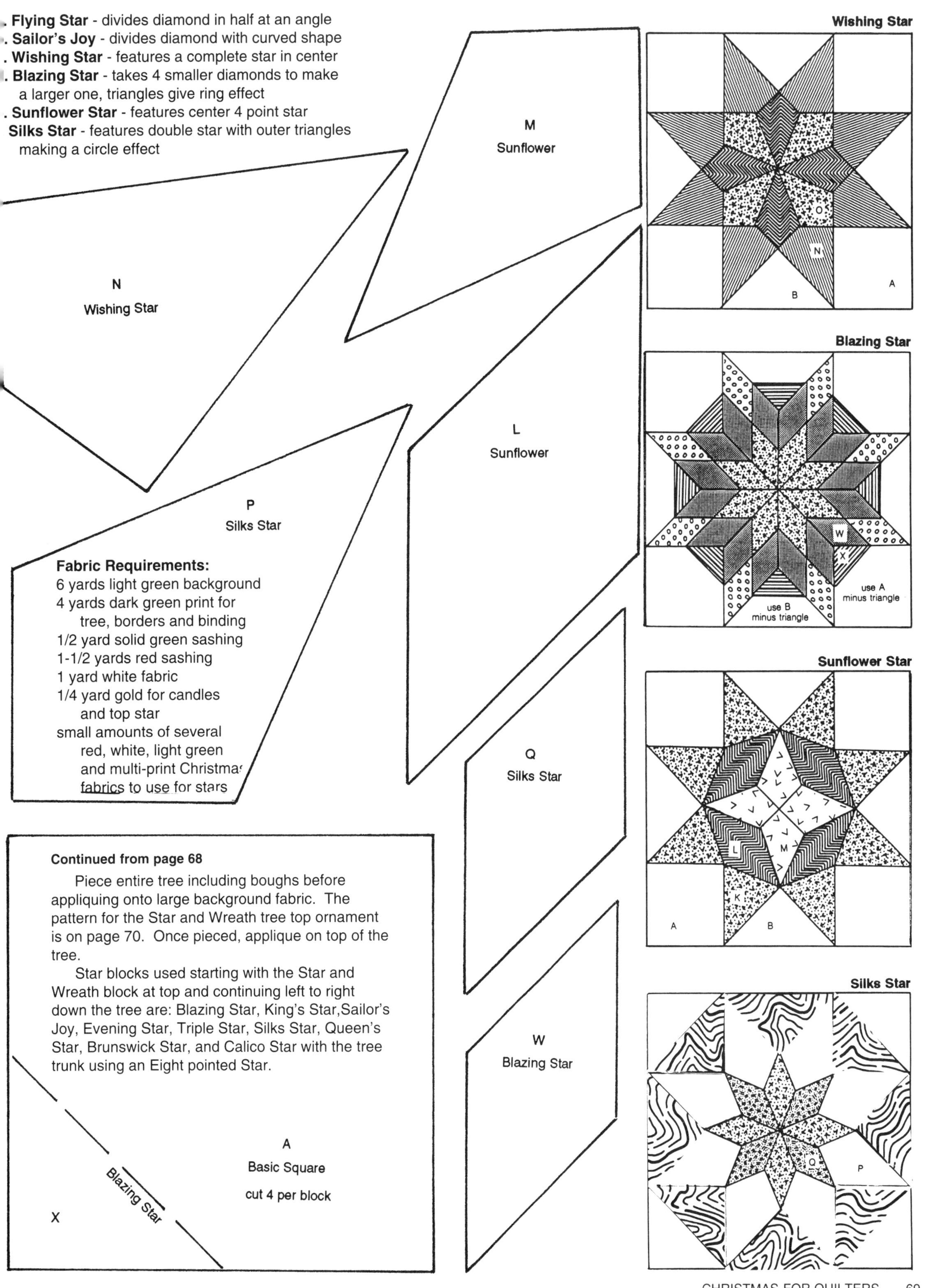

- **Flying Star** - divides diamond in half at an angle
- **Sailor's Joy** - divides diamond with curved shape
- **Wishing Star** - features a complete star in center
- **Blazing Star** - takes 4 smaller diamonds to make a larger one, triangles give ring effect
- **Sunflower Star** - features center 4 point star
- **Silks Star** - features double star with outer triangles making a circle effect

Fabric Requirements:

6 yards light green background
4 yards dark green print for tree, borders and binding
1/2 yard solid green sashing
1-1/2 yards red sashing
1 yard white fabric
1/4 yard gold for candles and top star
small amounts of several red, white, light green and multi-print Christmas fabrics to use for stars

Continued from page 68

Piece entire tree including boughs before appliquing onto large background fabric. The pattern for the Star and Wreath tree top ornament is on page 70. Once pieced, applique on top of the tree.

Star blocks used starting with the Star and Wreath block at top and continuing left to right down the tree are: Blazing Star, King's Star, Sailor's Joy, Evening Star, Triple Star, Silks Star, Queen's Star, Brunswick Star, and Calico Star with the tree trunk using an Eight pointed Star.

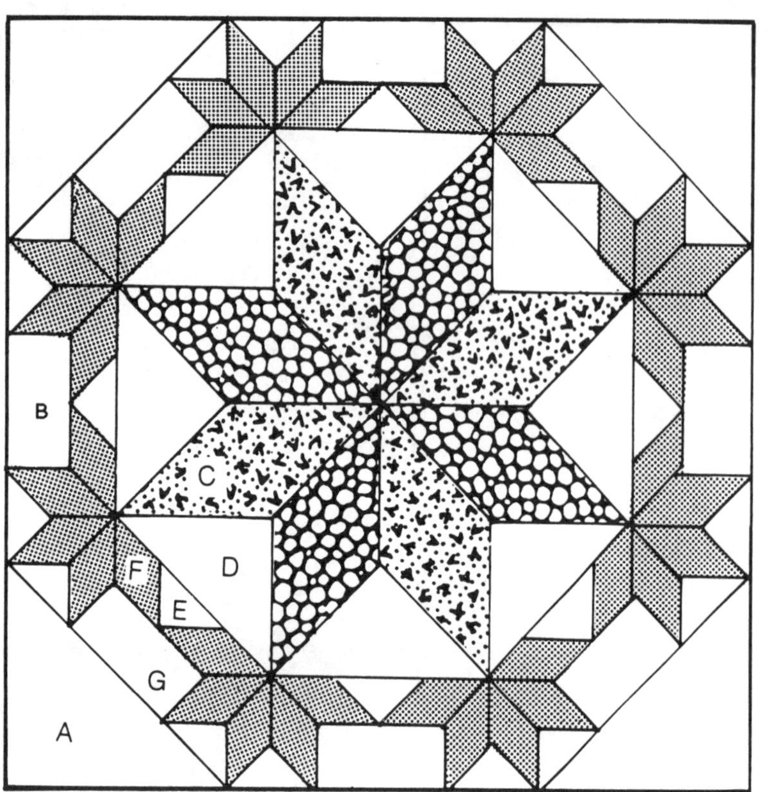

Star and Wreath

12 inch block
Add seam allowance, Difficult
Shown in color on page 34 and inside back cover

This block design is accredited to Nancy Cabot, a Chicago syndicated column from the 1930's. It is also calle Rising Star, but "Star and Wreath" seemed more appropriat for a Christmas book.

The 8 diamond center is bordered with 8 triangles to create the octagon shape. Next comes a row of eight smaller diamond clusters each made from five diamonds, giving a circle feeling to the block. Four triangles fill out corners to make the octagon shape a square. An assembly guide is included to aid in the progression of the pieces to fi the puzzle together.

A single block was made for use as the tree top star for the Christmas tree quilt. Quilt sketch is on page 68. Note the Star and Wreath Table Cover pictured in color on inside back cover to see the center variation.

See page 71 for a Star and Wreath variation where the center diamond is divided. The new diamond sketch is on the left.

F
cut 40
per block

C
cut 8 per block

B
cut 8 per block

A
cut 4 per block

E
cut 24
per block

D
cut 8 per block

Star and Wreath Table Cover

26 x 26 inches, Octagon
Add seam allowance, Difficult
Shown in color on inside back cover

The story of the six Holiday Quilters and their creative challenge is on page 32. As one of these quilters, Pat Nordmark of Delton, Michigan chose the most intricate of the pieced blocks offered. She prefers piecing and the smaller the better. The Star and Wreath block from page 70 was the initial 12 inch block. Pat decided that the center 8 diamonds were too large. Another popular traditional pattern, Flying Swallows divides diamonds even further. The diamond shape below illustrates the division process. It shows how diamonds are used and filled in with triangles to make a full diamond shape. The 12 inch block left Pat for the additions the next quilters would add. Squares and triangles were added to make the square shape. The third quilter enjoys applique, so decided to add holly leaves to the squares "G" previously added.

It was at this point, it reached me. As the fourth quilter, my assignment was to make final additions or borders to frame the quilt. To help emphasize the octagon shape of the initial block, the decision was made to extend the square to create an octagon outer edge. Pattern shapes are below.

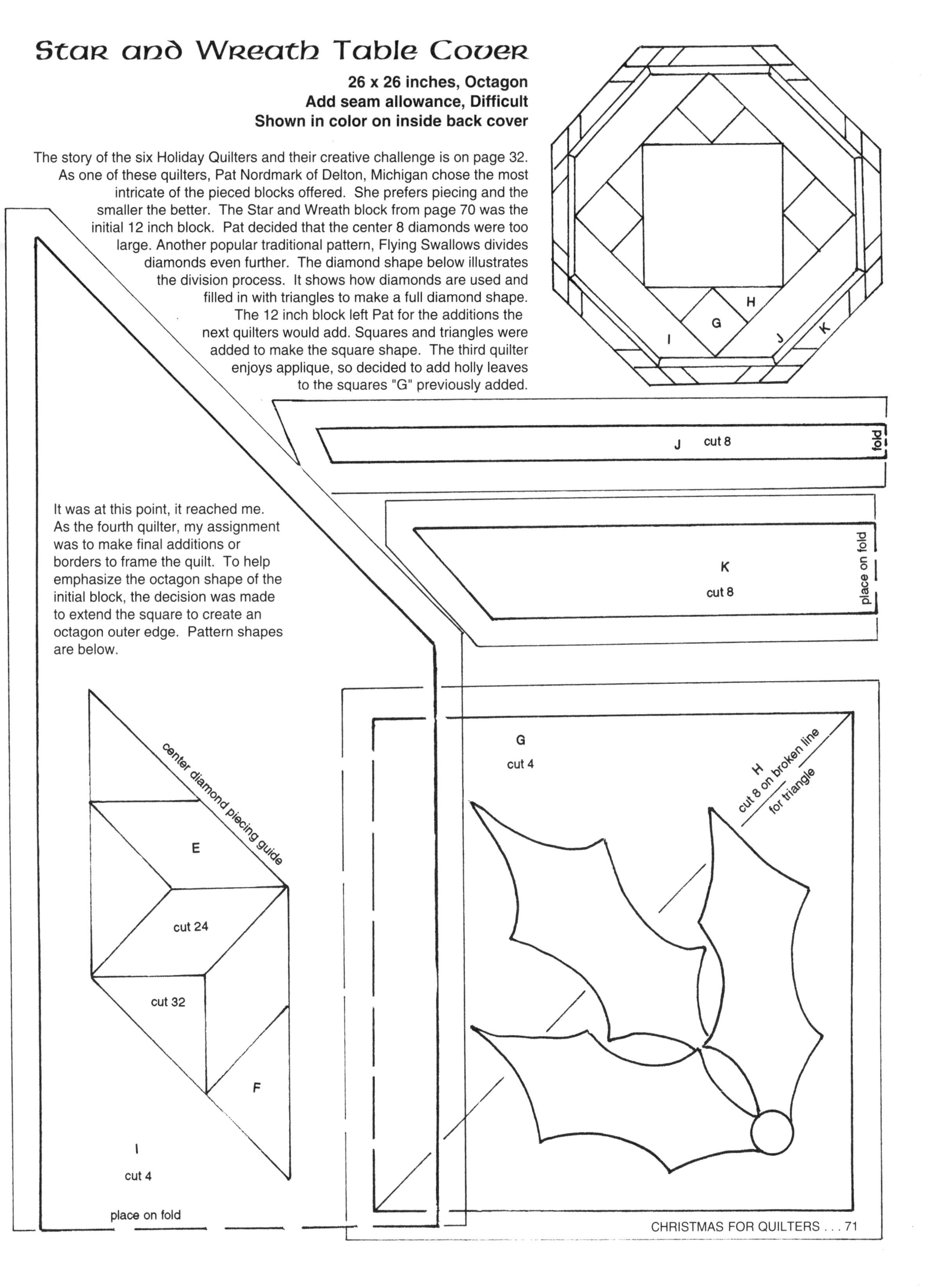

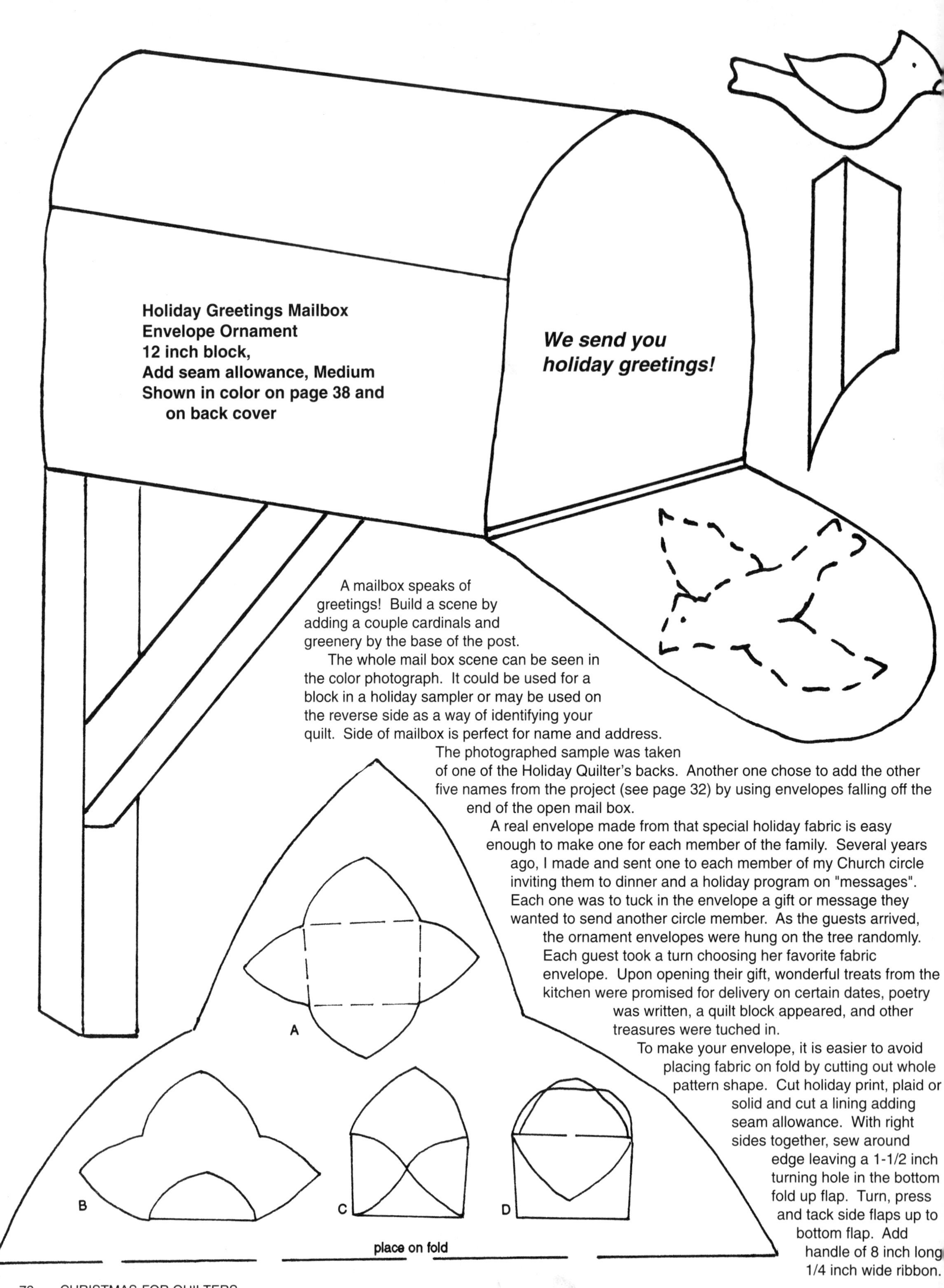

Holiday Greetings Mailbox
Envelope Ornament
12 inch block,
Add seam allowance, Medium
Shown in color on page 38 and on back cover

A mailbox speaks of greetings! Build a scene by adding a couple cardinals and greenery by the base of the post.

The whole mail box scene can be seen in the color photograph. It could be used for a block in a holiday sampler or may be used on the reverse side as a way of identifying your quilt. Side of mailbox is perfect for name and address.

The photographed sample was taken of one of the Holiday Quilter's backs. Another one chose to add the other five names from the project (see page 32) by using envelopes falling off the end of the open mail box.

A real envelope made from that special holiday fabric is easy enough to make one for each member of the family. Several years ago, I made and sent one to each member of my Church circle inviting them to dinner and a holiday program on "messages". Each one was to tuck in the envelope a gift or message they wanted to send another circle member. As the guests arrived, the ornament envelopes were hung on the tree randomly. Each guest took a turn choosing her favorite fabric envelope. Upon opening their gift, wonderful treats from the kitchen were promised for delivery on certain dates, poetry was written, a quilt block appeared, and other treasures were tuched in.

To make your envelope, it is easier to avoid placing fabric on fold by cutting out whole pattern shape. Cut holiday print, plaid or solid and cut a lining adding seam allowance. With right sides together, sew around edge leaving a 1-1/2 inch turning hole in the bottom fold up flap. Turn, press and tack side flaps up to bottom flap. Add handle of 8 inch long 1/4 inch wide ribbon.